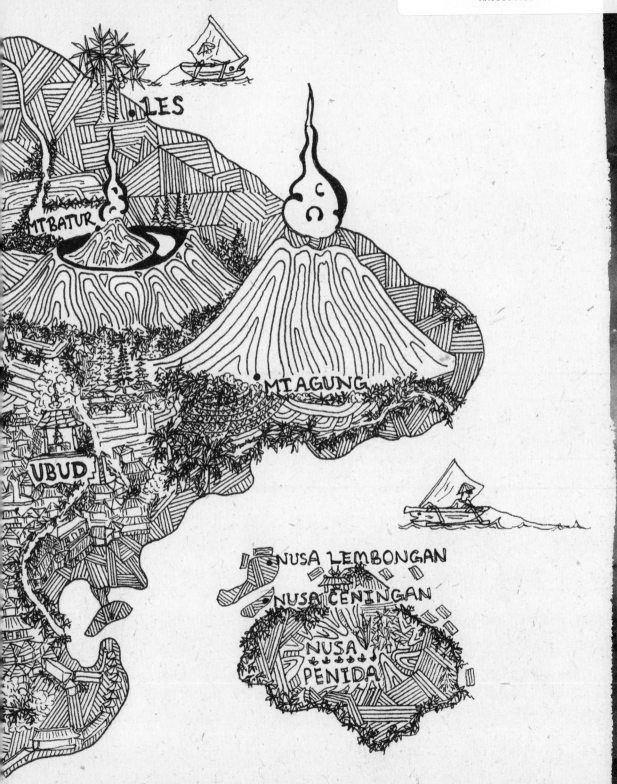

P A

Tjok Maya Kerthyasa and
I Wayan Kresna Yasa

O N

PAON

–

PAON

–

PAON

–

PAON

–

PAON

–

Hardie Grant

BOOKS

–

PAON

PAON IS THE
BALINESE
WORD FOR
KITCHEN.
IT IS DERIVED
FROM THE
WORD AON,
WHICH
MEANS ASHES.

More than a place to cook, a paon is an altar, an apothecary and a bridge to the natural world, where the hands of the cook

join forces with the earthly and heavenly elements to create nourishment, healing and connectivity to the universe.

INTRODUCTION

TJOK MAYA KERTHYASA

It's five o'clock in the morning. My niang (grandmother), Anak Agung Rai, is bent over her mudbrick stove with a bamboo pole in her right hand, stoking the freshly lit fire. 'It's better,' she says, 'to fill your mind with nice thoughts when you're cooking. Betara Brahma lives in the flames.'

In Hinduism, Brahma, The Creator, is part of the Trimurti (triple deity) alongside Wisnu, The Preserver, and Siwa, The Destroyer (see page 102 for more information). He's represented by the element of fire, and the Balinese hearth is one of his altars. Brahma isn't alone in the kitchen. Wisnu resides in the water pot and faucet nearby, and the two come together inside the feminine curves of the dangdang (clay rice cooker) – a symbol of the goddess of abundance, Dewi Sri. When the three forces combine, fire, water and the fruits of the earth, they create nourishment. 'This,' my grandmother says, 'is why we place offerings in the kitchen every day.'

My niang and I have been cooking together for four years now. Our conversations in her kitchen, a traditional open-air pavilion with carbonised terracotta roof tiles and a wood-fired cooktop, are what brought me home to Bali. Before that, I'd spent most of my life in Australia writing about nearly every other cuisine under the sun. On my trips home, I'd head straight for my niang's cooking – her smoke-tinged rice, delicate broths and flavour-packed sambals – and I'd wonder why the rest of the gastronomic world paid so little attention to Balinese food.

I now understand why. This kind of cooking is hard to capture in a snapshot. It's deeply tied to our Hindu–Buddhist faith, relies heavily on fresh ingredients (many of which are native to Bali's volcanic soil) and requires a hefty amount of peeling, chopping, pounding, grating and squeezing. My niang's generation learned and passed down knowledge orally, so the best recipes are rarely recorded on paper, and restaurants seldom have the time and tools to match the depth, complexity and zing of Bali's home kitchens. So, until recently, Balinese flavours have flown under the culinary radar, unexplored, for the most part, by chefs, food publications and hungry travellers. This book, I hope, will change that.

The recipes and stories on these pages represent practices that go beyond the creation of mere sustenance. They are part of a complex devotional system that dates back thousands of years and links humans with nature, with the gods and with ourselves. There's a popular term for this called Tri Hita Karana – a philosophical blueprint, if you like – for harmony among all beings, earthly and heavenly, natural and supernatural, seen and unseen. Food ties into this in the sense that in Bali, nothing is planted, picked or prepared without purpose. Agricultural traditions are centred around the cycles of the crops and the moon, and gods and goddesses are affiliated with the various elements that help us transform raw ingredients into nourishing and restorative dishes. Offerings in the form of cooked and uncooked rice, sacrificial meats and towering fruit and cake arrangements play a leading role in most ceremonial rituals. And so, through the simple act of engaging with food, the Balinese cook cements his or her place in the universe. We are practising an ancient and underrated form of yoga.

My niang drip-feeds me snippets of this wisdom with every cook we do together. 'Well-composed spices will balance you on the inside,' she might say, or, 'Use your hands and all your senses. Put your energy into the dish.'

I take her advice seriously – she's a culinary heavyweight with more than seventy years of kitchen experience. My niang's mother passed suddenly when she was just a girl. It's hard to say exactly how old she was (the men and women of her generation don't care much for the Gregorian calendar), but we believe that she was still on the cusp of womanhood. Her father, unable to care for his daughter, sent her and her brother to serve at the Puri (noble court) of Ubud. 'He left me at the gate,' she once told me, 'and I never saw him again.' From that moment, my niang was in the hands of strangers, but she found refuge, eventually, by the warmth of the hearth. At the Puri, she cooked for guests and elders, for the community and during ceremonial events. She was in many ways the leader of the palace kitchen – Puri Ubud's own young and charismatic head chef.

After some time in the palace, she married my grandfather Tjokorda Ngurah, a palace elder more than fifty years her senior. He had multiple wives and my niang was the youngest and the last. It's safe to say that there was little romance between the pair, but there was a deep exchange of food knowledge. My niang is a naturally talented cook – one of my aunts once told me she has magic in her fingertips – and my grandfather was a scholar, magician and artist, and a culinary master in his own right. He studied and wrote Balinese sastra or literature, carved sacred masks, statues and idols, and lived by the teachings of Tantra, the Sanskrit epic Ramayana and the fourteenth-century Javanese Hindu-Buddhist text, the Sutasoma. His fascination with the spiritual world would sometimes lead him into month-long spells of solitude on the ancestral land that I now call home. Sometimes, he would meditate, motionless, for three days, only to rise and resume his daily life as if nothing had happened. Tukak taught his young wife how to combine spices, cook with rare plants and proteins and apply spiritual depth to her dishes. She quotes him regularly in the kitchen, and every night before bed she massages her arms and legs with a medicinal oil – replete with grasshoppers, tiny local limes and eleven other roots, leaves, barks and flowers – that he taught her to make. 'This is why I'm stronger than you,' she likes to tease me with a betel-stained grin.

The paon is my spiritual safe haven. Through cooking and eating, I've been drawn closer to the rhythm of the island. It's helped me decode the culture, become more respectful of the landscape and understand the importance of presence, process and purpose – not only behind the pans, but also across many other areas of my life. It's also driven me to record and share the real flavours of Bali, the stuff beyond the eateries, beach bars and hotel kitchens – the dishes most people don't see.

I know Wayan Kresna Yasa feels the same way. We met around five years ago when I was interviewing him about Ijen – the sustainable seafood restaurant he'd just opened at the Potato Head complex on Bali's south-west coast. Wayan's cooking at Ijen was clean, honest and extremely clever. He grilled line-caught fish in banana leaves and served them with punchy spice pastes inspired by the flavours of his home island, Nusa Penida. The leftover fish scales were powdered and baked into moreish crackers, not dissimilar to the local variety known as kerupuk. Wayan's kitchens (he was in charge of six at the time) were designed to generate as little waste as possible, so vegetable off-cuts would make their way into warm salads or pickles, and turmeric skins would be fermented into a type of gently carbonated root beer. He added a subtle contemporary edge to local flavours and made them shine – there wasn't a watered-down nasi goreng in sight.

During COVID-19, Wayan's restaurants, along with many other businesses in the island's tourist industry, closed their doors temporarily. My work started to dry up, too, and eventually we decided to join forces and write this book. We've included family heirlooms from our own kitchens, as well as recipes from other parts of the island, such as night markets, temple kitchens, farms and warungs (local eateries). If you've never visited Bali, we hope these dishes will inspire you to make the trip. If you're Balinese or already well-versed in the cuisine, we hope you appreciate our efforts to share the island's flavours in a way that reflects its very unique spirit – bright, intriguing and laced with deeper meaning.

I WAYAN KRESNA YASA

A food journalist once asked me, 'How do you feel about the way the rest of the world perceives or views Balinese food?' My answer was simple: 'They don't.' There is a void of information and resources about our food beyond Bali's borders, and most people outside of our small island have little to no idea what Balinese food is supposed to taste and feel like. With this book, Maya and I hope to change that. We hope people outside of Bali will form a deeper understanding of Balinese cuisine and flavours, and grasp the deeper meanings behind our food dishes and rituals.

So many significant moments or memories in my life are focused around food – learning to fish and forage to help feed my family, learning to farm seaweed to earn money to feed the family, and literally learning to feed my family by helping my mother with the cooking. Cooking has never been about earning money for me, it's always been about my love for self and others.

It may sound trite to say that it doesn't matter how much money one has, but in the time and place where I grew up that was not just hyperbole. I was born on Nusa Penida, a small, arid island just off the southern coast of mainland Bali. When I was a child, Nusa Penida was still isolated from the mainland, and the food we had available to us was only what we could farm, forage and catch. My family lived simply, relying on the resources available in our environment and climate. I learned from a young age that food was security and food was communal. In my family and village, we understood that sharing our food harvests with those around us was essential. We shared with each other so that all of us would have a bit (even just a tiny bit) of everything the island had to offer.

Food could also be love or medicine, and sometimes it was both. There is a story my aunties like to tell about the year the small mango that grows on my island helped to save my life. When I was six or seven years old, I had fallen ill with what was most likely Hepatitis A. Without a doctor or hospital on the island at the time, my family didn't have a precise diagnosis or access to Western medicine. So, my aunties cared for me in the only way they knew how to: with food. They fed me pisang mas (golden bananas), believed to have special medicinal effects. There was only one complication with this remedy; pisang mas do not grow on Nusa Penida. My aunt had to travel to the mainland every few days on a small wooden jukung (outrigger canoe) supply boat and bring her 'currency' with her to trade for the coveted golden banana. This currency was grown on her own land – mangga lembongan, a small, sweet mango that can be found on Nusa Penida but not on mainland Bali and is therefore considered a delicacy. My aunt traded her mangoes for the golden bananas, which she then brought back to Nusa Penida to nurse me back to health. Now, I cannot say whether or not these bananas are the reason I recovered, it could have been time that healed me or my aunt's love, but in any case, I am still here to tell the tale.

My concept of food really started to expand when I was thirteen years old and my dad took a job as a transport boat captain. I no longer saw food only in terms of survival or community, I began to experience it as a new adventure, something fun to look forward to where new experiences awaited me. Once a week, my dad travelled for work between Nusa Penida and Bali, and each time he returned home to the village, he would bring us kids a culinary treat from the mainland – a new food to try, a different dish to taste or a sweet jaja (traditional cake or sweet) to revel in. My culinary curiosity was endless, and a passion for food and food adventures was born.

Years later, I remember what was going through my mind when I decided to apply to US culinary schools: I really wanted to introduce the world to Balinese cuisine. The reason people come to Bali, I think, is primarily to enjoy the culture, so I began to wonder how we could carry our culture beyond Bali's borders and into the homes of people through Balinese food. The first time I had the opportunity to bring a taste of Bali to a popular US restaurant was when the chef allowed me to add Sambal tomat (page 84) to flavour a dish. I'll never forget it. I was so happy that I promised to not leave his restaurant until I had finished my culinary school studies, a promise that I kept.

My parents back in the village didn't understand why I wanted to go to America to study cooking all those years ago. My dad said I should 'just stay home' and learn cooking from my mother. I tried to tell my dad that things are different and that this was a big deal for me, but sadly, I don't think he ever fully grasped my reasons for moving so far away before he passed away. You know, when you've been in the US for several years and return home to your small fishing village, people there expect you to bring money home, and here I was bringing home nothing but a culinary school diploma! Of course my dad was happy and proud of his son, but it's safe to say he wasn't really impressed.

But today, more than a decade has passed and COVID-19 has impacted the entire world, including Bali, and the restaurants I oversee were shuttered for more than a year. Nevertheless, I have something to celebrate, because the pandemic brought a resurgence of the traditional farming and fishing practices to my home island of Nusa Penida. Before the pandemic, I didn't think it was possible to 'go back in time' and see the island as it used to be, ever again, but that is precisely what has happened. Now is the perfect time to do a deep-dive into my Balinese culinary heritage and tell our stories, while the stories are still here to tell.

Throughout this book, we have documented the recipes and stories of our food heritage, and Maya and I are excited to share the wisdom and knowledge from our mothers' and grandmothers' paons. More importantly, however, we have shared why our cuisine is meaningful to us in every way — meaningful to our health, to our spirit, to our communities and to our longevity. We Balinese food lovers welcome you to our tables and our temples, which to some of us are one and the same thing.

ELEMENTAL COOKING: INTRODUCING THE PAON

Once upon a time, not very long ago, most of us lived in family compounds made up of various living structures. Many of us still do. In these types of settings, each building is thoughtfully positioned based on the directional laws of Uluteben. Put very simply, the most sacred part of the home, the family temple, is oriented towards the mountains and the rising sun in a direction known as kaja-kangin. The more impure areas are placed in the kelod, or seaward-facing direction of the home. This could be north, east, south or west on a conventional compass depending on what part of the island you're standing on. The simplest way to wrap your head around it is to imagine all the 'clean', or pure, spaces facing the great mountains, and the 'unclean' spaces positioned towards the sea. This is not to say the sea is unholy. It is simply an observation that the coast is positioned below the mountains, where we feel closest to god.

The paon is one of the kelod-facing parts of the home. It's a place of hard labour and elemental rawness – soot clings to the roof tiles, animals are sacrificed on the spot and the floor is often left as bare earth. At the same time, it's somewhat of an altar. The energies that reside here are routinely appeased with offerings and one is always encouraged to enter the space in a state of calm. So, it's a brilliant example of the theme of

duality in Bali – how something, or somewhere, can be both pure and impure, dark and light, sacred and worldly. We embrace it all.

A classic kitchen structure is usually wall-less and simply outfitted with a low workbench, a large water tub and a jalikan (wood-fired stove). A cupboard stands in the place of a fridge (Balinese food, after all, is designed to be eaten fresh and is rarely kept for longer than a day), and baskets and containers made from coconut shells might hang from the rafters, keeping salt, sugar and other ingredients safe from ants and other hungry visitors.

Real Balinese food gets its depth and earthiness from the natural elements of the paon. The wood fire creates smoke that seeps through porous clay pots, woks and woven bamboo steamers into the cooking. Bamboo poles and coconut shell ladles are used for stirring and scooping; and palm fronds and banana leaves serve as plates, covers and wrapping. Any spillages are quickly soaked up by the earthen floor, and scraps are usually divided between the pigs, dogs and chickens of the household. So, nature makes its way into every dish in a subtle but indisputable way, and at the same time, food finds its way back into nature.

Although contemporary kitchens with their various bells and whistles – gas stoves, rice cookers, refrigerators and metal cookware – play their part in modern island life, true paons are still favoured among serious Balinese cooks. Some family compounds even have both. And in many cases, nowadays, modern and ancient cooking tools and techniques are combined to bring Balinese flavours to life faster and more efficiently.

HOW TO USE THIS BOOK

Not all Balinese dishes are created equal. Some are reserved for offerings or rituals, others only appear on the menu for special celebrations, and the rest are for everyday nourishment.

Our food can be as modest as a plate of fresh pineapple with sea salt and chopped chillies, or as complex as minced duck massaged with grated coconut and spices, then pressed around bamboo skewers, wrapped in banana leaves and grilled slowly over coconut husks.

In our eyes, all of these riffs on Balinese cooking – from the simple to the spectacular – are worthy of praise and preservation.

In the pages that follow, you'll find recipes and stories from people, places and traditions that have inspired us, as well as advice on how to incorporate some of the practices of our kitchens into yours.

Let the essays guide you to a better understanding of Balinese culture and the deeper meaning of Balinese cooking – the philosophies, rituals and elements that give it purpose and soul. Then apply this wisdom through the recipes, turning it into something tangible: food designed to nourish, connect us to our consciousness and express our gratitude to the universe.

THE ESSENTIALS
–
THE ESSENTIALS
–
THE ESSENTIALS
–
THE ESSENTIALS
–
THE ESSENTIALS
–
THE ESSENTIALS
–
THE

ESSENTIAL EQUIPMENT

Balinese cooking is all about chopping, grating, hand-tossing and pounding (see page 36 for traditional tools and equipment). It's best to process spices by finely chopping them (rajang-style, see page 53) or pounding them in a mortar and pestle. The grinding action of the mortar and pestle ensures all the juices and flavours are released and well-incorporated into the dish. To create the dishes in this book successfully you'll need:

- large mortar and pestle
- large mixing bowl
- steamer pot with a steamer basket
- sharp and sturdy cleaver
- box grater
- microplane

STERILISING JARS

To sterilise jars, wash them in hot soapy water or in the dishwasher, then place them in the oven set to 150°C (300°F) until completely dry.

BALINESE FLAVOURS

If you get the chance to visit Bali, there are a few things you should bring back home: sea salt, palm sugar and coconut oil. Some of the best stuff comes from Tejakula, Amed and Dawan in the island's north-east. Quality bottled coconut oil is easy to find all around the island these days, even in supermarkets.

Ingredients: There are some ingredients that are essential for Balinese cooking and for the recipes in this book. Most can be found at good Asian grocers, supermarkets and online, but others are a bit trickier to find outside Bali. For more information on sourcing, plant varieties and substitutes, head to the Glossary (page 273) and Rare edible plants (page 127).

- Asian shallot
- Candlenut
- Chilli
- Coconut
- Coriander seeds
- Galangal
- Garlic
- Ginger
- Lemongrass
- Lesser galangal
- Lime
- Tamarind
- Turmeric
- Salam leaves
- Shrimp paste

Base: The word base (pronounced bah-surr) refers to spices or mixtures of spice. Intricate pastes, seasonings and finely chopped roots, bulbs and rhizomes are the foundation of Balinese cooking – we expand on this on page 44. If you're planning to cook Balinese food regularly, it's good to have several batches of your favourite base pastes and mixtures ready to go. Like most of the recipes in the book, base combinations are best made fresh, but you can make them in bulk and store them in the freezer. The traditional art of hand-working your food adds a rhythmic element to the cooking. We also believe it connects the cook and the ingredients on an energetic level, where the dish becomes an offering laced with love and intention. So, skip the food processor (as tempting as it might be), acquaint yourself with mortar and pestle and allow your spirit to spill into every pound or slice. As a rule, you can get away with substituting one fresh spice for a powder when making base (using a 3:1 ratio – the powder should be one third of the fresh spice weight), but no more than one, or it will affect the consistency and flavour of the dish.

PREPARING INGREDIENTS

Sambal: While base spice combinations are cooked into a dish, sambals are normally served alongside them. Few Balinese can eat, let alone live, without these spicy condiments. They are to us what salsas are to Mexico, or what pickles might be to India. Sometimes, sambals are tossed through dishes such as urab (see page 132) and Ayam sisit (page 152) to bring extra heat and punch. Regardless of whether a dish already contains sambal or not, one (or sometimes a few) will be served as a side with every meal. This book contains raw, steamed and fried sambals alike. Some of them are sweet and mild, some are hot and pungent, others are smoky and caramelised. Pick your favourites and pair them with whatever you like – there are no set rules in the sambal game.

Candlenuts: Please note that candlenuts are toxic when they're raw and must be cooked before consumption. To roast, place the candlenuts on a baking tray and bake them in the oven at 163°C/325°F for about 10 minutes, or until lightly brown in colour.

Roots: Galangal should always be peeled. Most cooks will just wash ginger and turmeric, but if you prefer them peeled, that's fine, too (you can use a spoon when peeling roots to waste less of the flesh). Lesser galangal, however, is rarely peeled as the skin contains a good portion of its flavour – we recommend washing it well and leaving the skin on.

Chillies: Make sure you wash your hands well after handling chillies, and be mindful not to touch your eyes or other sensitive areas afterwards as it can burn. See page 274 for more information on the types of chillies used in Balinese cooking and their substitutes.

Coconuts: Dried or desiccated coconut is not a suitable substitute in any of the recipes in this book. We also strongly recommend you make your own santen (coconut milk) and oil (see the coconut guide on pages 90–7 for recipes and more information).

Palm sugar: For the recipes in From the Land, we recommend using coconut palm sugar. For the seafood recipes, try lontar sugar if you can find it. Palm sugar is almost always grated or finely chopped, so avoid granulated palm sugar unless the recipe specifically calls for it. The traditional way is to finely shave off the palm sugar using a knife, but you can also use the larger holes of a box grater. Head to the Glossary (page 273) for more information on sugars from different types of palms.

Banana leaves: Asian supermarkets and Thai grocers will often have fresh and frozen banana leaves. If you use frozen leaves, simply defrost them at room temperature before you start cooking. They take around 15 minutes to defrost and can be used in the same way as fresh leaves once they're ready. Sometimes, you'll want to soften the banana leaf to make it pliable and easy to work with. To do this, you either steam it for 5 minutes or microwave it on a medium setting for 20 seconds. The goal is to get it soft and flexible. See the opposite page for general instructions on how to work with banana leaves. Specific tips, such as folding techniques, are provided with the individual recipes.

To make a banana leaf parcel, place two pieces of banana leaf on top of each other, with the bottom leaf's top (glossy) side facing the bench and the top leaf's glossy side facing you. The veins of both leaves should face in the same direction.

Place the filling in the middle of the leaves going along the grain. Banana leaves can tear when you fold them against the grain, so it is important to use the veins of the leaf as a guide when placing the filling and rolling the leaf.

There are many ways to fold banana leaf parcels, and most are fastened at the end with toothpicks. There are also more advanced folding methods, such as Tum bebek (page 154).

PREPARATION METHODS

Crushing: When a recipe calls for an ingredient to be crushed, simply place it on a chopping board and press down on it with the flat side of a knife or cleaver blade. Alternatively, you could give it a gentle pound in a mortar and pestle. This technique is used in dishes where you want to extract the flavour of a specific ingredient without incorporating its texture – the chillies in Nyoman's rujak (page 165), for example.

Knotting: Knotted lemongrass and pandan leaves are used as aromatics in many dishes. To knot lemongrass, simply remove the green outer part of the stem, cut off the brittle end and gently bruise the fleshier white end with a mortar and pestle or a knife (using the instructions above). Tie a firm, neat knot on the stem in the centre, and throw it into the likes of Balung (page 246) for perfume and flavour. Pandan leaves can be knotted and added straight in. Remove before serving.

Toasting and roasting: Roots and spices can be lightly dry-toasted in a frying pan over a medium heat for 5 minutes, then set aside to cool. Candlenuts are mildly toxic when consumed raw and need to be cooked before eating or even tasting a dish they are in (see page 26). Roasting the candlenuts also increases and refines their flavour, making for an umami quality that spills into the dish.

Cooking with fire: All Balinese cooks and food enthusiasts will agree that the best dishes are cooked the traditional way: over a wood fire. There are a few reasons for this. Firstly, it adds depth to the food, lacing it with a smoky, rustic, earthy flavour. Rice is particularly delicious when it's cooked this way. Secondly, it connects the cook and the food to the raw element of fire, which in many traditional medicinal schools is believed to be beneficial for digestion and vitality. So, try and cook with a gas flame at the very least. If you have access to a fire pit or charcoal grill, even better. For dishes that normally require grilling or smoking, a barbecue or oven can be fine substitutes also. We've included instructions for how to use modern kitchen equipment in the recipes where appropriate.

USE YOUR HANDS

Cook with them. Eat with them. Let them feel for ripeness, texture and seasonings.

Intuition is a huge part of Balinese cooking. Veteran cooks can tell if a dish lacks seasoning just from the way it looks, feels and smells.

Mixing, massaging and squeezing with our hands connects us to our food in a special way. We learn to speak the language of our ingredients, understanding the subtleties of their biological composition, feeling when they are ready without needing to taste.

As we cook with our hands, we spill our own thoughts and intentions into every dish. When we work directly with the raw elements, such as a wood fire, we combine our own human intelligence with the life-giving powers of the universe, the prana (energy) from the water, fire and air that helps bring food to life.

ON SERVING

We rarely cook standalone dishes and most of the recipes on these pages are meant to be eaten as part of a larger spread or with a side of steamed rice and sambal, at the very least.

When you're planning out a larger menu, think about colour, flavour and texture. Try and include something soft, something soupy, something with a bit of crunch, something spicy, something to cool the palate and something sweet. The idea is to create balance on the plate, which, we believe, translates through to various parts of the body, mind and soul.

In saying that, there are no set rules. We traditionally cook based on the availability of ingredients in nature, so if all you feel like is a bowl of sautéed fern tips with some roasted taro on the side, go for it and enjoy every mouthful.

Sample spreads
1. Gecok (page 147), with Urab timun (page 132), Paku tumis (page 138), Nasi putih (page 111), Sambal matah (page 76), Sambal goreng (page 75) and Es kuwud (page 231) for dessert.
2. Pepes be pasih (page 187), Gurita suna cekuh (page 195), Nasi sela (page 115), Urab gedang (page 204) and Sambal poh (page 184).

PRIVATE DINING

In Bali, everyday eating is a solitary act rather than a big family affair. We go to the paon and organise a plate of food when it pleases us, normally enjoying it in silence and away from others.

We announce that we're eating in the hope that the people around us will grant us a moment to consume our food in peace – which they always do. Many of us will put together a small offering called a saiban – a pinch of everything we're eating on a square of banana leaf – to our kanda empat (four energetic siblings), who we believe guard us, guide us and keep us away from trouble. It's important, as you can imagine, that we nourish them well.

On special occasions, food is laid out on platters lined with banana leaves, which are conveniently waxy and waterproof, making washing up a much easier task. Even at family feasts or temple ceremonies, people tend to take their food and eat it quietly on their own, but there is definitely much more of a communal energy.

There are a few regional traditions that bring Balinese diners together; for megibung, a tradition from Karangasem in the island's east, for example, small groups of diners sit cross-legged around banana leaves piled high with rice, sates, vegetables and condiments designed to be shared. But for the most part, dining is a very personal practice that is encouraged to be carried out mindfully, much like the cooking process itself.

TRADITIONAL BALINESE COOKING EQUIPMENT

PAYUK

Here are some of the key players of the paon – the traditional implements that help grate, slice, pound, mince, grill, steam and fry Balinese food into existence. We've listed them here with suggestions for how you can substitute them with conventional cookware. Plastic has no place in a true paon. Banana leaves, coconut shell bowls and containers and baskets woven out of bamboo are used for wrapping and covering foods and storing ingredients. Most dishes are consumed on the day they are cooked, so try and reduce the amount of plastic you use by adopting this principle. If you happen to be in Indonesia, we recommend you head to your nearest market or a traditional home appliances store (known locally as a toko prabot) to source as many of these tools as you can. They'll take the flavours and textures of your cooking to whole new heights.

PANGORENGAN

BATU BASE

DANGDANG, KUKUSAN AND KEKEB

PAYUK

These big-bellied pots are made from red clay and were traditionally used to cook everything from rice to water to stews. Today, most people use aluminium pots and dangdangs in place of clay payuks. If you're cooking over gas, electric plates or induction, use a good-quality stainless steel, cast-iron or copper pot or saucepan instead.

PANGORENGAN

A traditional large frying pan made from red clay. Pangorengan pans are used to toast spices, reduce liquids, shallow-fry cakes and meats, sauté vegetables and more. Being clay, they're not particularly suitable for electric or induction stovetops but can be easily replaced with a wok.

BATU BASE

The mortar and pestle is the hardest-working tool in the paon. When used for spices it is referred to as a batu base. There's a shallow type with raised edges for grinding, known as a penguyegan or pengulekan, and a deeper sort better suited to pounding, called a lesung (mortar) and lu (pestle). Most kitchens will have at least one of the two, if not both, fashioned out of strong volcanic rock. There's really no real substitute for the batu base. It brings both flavour and rhythm to the cooking process, and the act of grinding and pounding is highly meditative. It unifies the cook with the ingredients, encouraging presence and connection. It also works the spices in a way that maximises their output – pressing the juices out of them, as opposed to just slicing them the way a blender or food processor might do. It's also worth noting that ingredients ground in the batu base only make contact with stone and not metal, which helps retain and even enhance their natural flavours. So if you're really in a rush, we'll forgive you for using a food processor once or twice, but we encourage you to embrace the batu base and take note of how it transforms not only the final result of your cooking but the process as a whole.

DANGDANG, KUKUSAN AND KEKEB

Rice is traditionally cooked in a conical kukusan basket that sits over a dangdang pot. A clay kekeb lid holds the steam in and the whole thing bubbles away over a wood fire for about 15 minutes before it's taken off the heat, steeped in the hot water that was steaming it, stirred to loosen the grains and then steamed once more until the rice is fat, fluffy and soft enough to press between two fingers. Kukusan baskets are also great for steaming cakes, leaf-wrapped meats, sweet potatoes and roots and corms such as cassava and taro. Natural fibres play a big role in Balinese cooking, so we suggest using any kind of bamboo steamer if you can't find a traditional one. Otherwise, a regular steamer pot will do the job just fine.

PANGIKIHAN

PANGIKIHAN AND GOBED

Every serious cook will have two kinds of graters. There's the pangikihan: a long wood or aluminium board dotted with tiny nails or round, punched holes, designed for grating coconut into a fine, powder-like consistency. The second is a gobed or pangukuran: a wider grater for coarser results. Use the wider holes of a regular box grater in place of a gobed. For the pangikihan, use the finest grater you can find – such as a microplane – or the smallest holes of your box grater. You want the coconut to come out soft enough to squeeze into Santen (coconut milk, see page 94) and fine enough to sprinkle over cakes and desserts, sort of like powdery parmesan.

CEDOK

There are probably more than fifteen different household tools made from coconut shells. The cedok is one of the most prominent. It's a deep ladle made with a curved coconut wood handle, used for scooping water into rice and other dishes as you cook. It can be replaced with a bamboo or wooden ladle. We don't recommend using plastic ladles and cooking spoons.

CEDOK

PANE

The big-batch, multi-ingredient culinary style of the paon calls for mixing vessels to be as large as possible. Clay pane pots are used for mixing, marinating and soaking – even the washing up. You can use a large glass, ceramic or stainless-steel bowl instead.

PANE

TIUK AND TALENAN

Balinese cooks peel using a super sharp tiuk, a small knife, sliding the blade away from the body using the index finger as a guide. The tiuk chops, slices and trims – it's the paring knife of the paon. It's helped along by the chunky talenan (chopping board) made from a whole piece of wood, sometimes a dissection of a teak, tamarind or jackfruit tree, that provides height and a solid foundation for all the knife work required to bring Balinese food to life. Replace a talenan with the thickest wooden board you can find. Most Balinese chopping is done from a seated position, so if you decide to go down this route, try elevating your chopping board on a pile of books to make the process more comfortable.

TIUK AND TALENAN

KATUNG

The open-aired paon attracts many curious visitors – dogs, cats, birds and insects alike. These woven bamboo baskets, sometimes called keranjang gantung, are designed to hang from the roof beams to keep food off the ground. They are normally hung with string made from coconut palm fibres that ants can't climb down. These days, most people use a cupboard or a fridge for storage, or they'll leave the food on the dining table, covered with a bamboo or plastic food cover to keep the flies at bay.

SOKASI

These woven bamboo baskets are used to store cooked rice, spices, bulbs, root vegetables and other ingredients – a portable pantry of sorts. Sometimes they're used for transporting offerings. They aren't essential but are useful for organising your base staples and keeping cooked rice fluffy and warm.

SIDI

A woven strainer made from bamboo, mainly used for rinsing rice and vegetables. Use a fine-mesh sieve in its place.

BELAKAS

These knives are heavy bladed, super sharp and mainly used to mince and chop meat. Some cooks also use them to finely chop leaves and spices. Rhythmic chopping is such an important part of Balinese cooking, so if you're on the island or have a chance to visit, we highly recommend getting your own belakas made at a pande (blacksmith). Otherwise, substitute with a cleaver.

KATUNG
SOKASI
SIDI

BELAKAS

MEASUREMENTS AND CONVERSIONS

Recipes are presented in grams and millilitres, with conversions for ounces and cups included (the latter where practicable). Some ingredients are given as spoon measures, amounts or length, depending on their type.

This book uses 20 ml (¾ fl oz) tablespoons and 250 ml (8½ fl oz) cup measures. US/UK tablespoon measures are 15 ml (½ fl oz). US cups are 240 ml (8 fl oz), so US cooks should be generous in their cup measurements; in the UK, one imperial cup is 285 ml (9½ fl oz), so UK cooks should be scant in their cup measurements.

Vegetables are medium-sized unless otherwise indicated.

Oven temperatures are for conventional ovens. If using a fan-forced oven, decrease the temperature by 20°C (70°F).

FOUNDATIONS

–

FOUNDATIONS

–

FOUNDATIONS

–

FOUNDATIONS

–

FOUNDATIONS

–

FOUNDATIONS

–

FOUNDATIONS

–

FOUNDATIONS

SPICES,

SAMBALS,

CONDIMENTS

AND OTHER

ESSENTIALS

YOU ARE WHAT YOU EAT

SPICES AND SELECTIVE EATING

There's no such thing as a slow morning in the paon. There are fires to light, birds to butcher and enough rice needs to be steamed to feed the family for the day. Coconuts are hacked, grated and squeezed into coconut milk and cooking oil. And, most importantly, there are spices to pound.

Base (spice) – pronounced bah-surr – is the backbone of Balinese cooking. Turmeric, black and white peppercorns, chillies, garlic, red (Asian) shallots, coriander seeds and various strains of ginger and galangal lend their aroma, colour and heat to most of the island's traditional dishes. They come together in a variety of pastes – always made from fresh ingredients and pounded in a stone batu base (mortar and pestle). There's Base genep (page 50), the complete spice paste that forms the foundation of many meat-based dishes; Suna cekuh (page 56), a punchy seasoning made from garlic and lesser galangal gently fried in coconut oil; and Base wangen (page 54), a combination of long peppercorns, nutmeg, several types of ginger, coriander seeds and candlenuts that provide wangi (aroma). When spices and aromatics are not made into pastes, they're finely chopped rajang-style (see page 53) or simply sliced and tossed through sautées and stir-fries.

The rhythmic thunk of the batu base signals the start of the day in many family compounds. The designated cooks of the household peel, chop and pound kilograms of spices and aromatics every week – without the aid of base, food is considered bland, incomplete and decidedly inedible. But the Balinese devotion to spice comes down to much more than just flavour– the mastering of Sad Rasa (the six fundamental tastes: bitter, hot, sweet, salty, sour and astringent) through the articulation of spices is also a symbolic act of creating harmony. The idea is that we should taste and embrace all the flavours of life, as each plays a unique and vital role in the beat of the universe and our health.

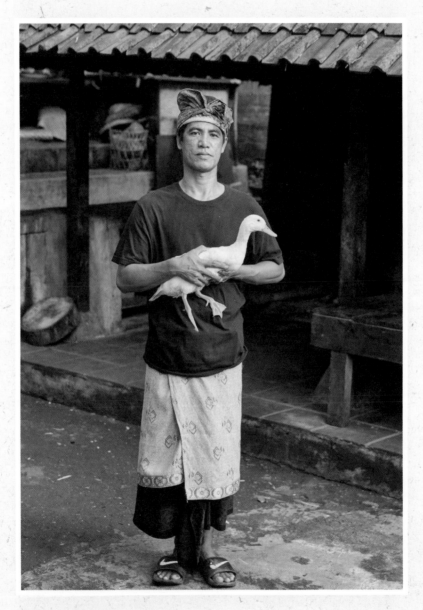

*Above: Nyoman holding a duck about
to be cooked for a ceremonial feast.
Left: Chillies, tamarind and sliced
jicama at the ready for the preparation
of rujak bengkuang.*

Above: Wayan's mother holding a young Balinese heritage pig; the piglet will be sold for ceremonial use in the village.

Harmony tastes different from one village, or kitchen, to another – in central Bali it's notably complex and earthy; in the island's north and west, chillies reign supreme. Some cooks add terasi (shrimp paste) for extra pungency, while others include lemongrass for perfume. Different meats and vegetables call for tweaks to the formula: for example, pork dishes might have lots of lesser galangal, while chicken and fish are known to pair best with ginger.

The base formulas also double as home remedies. They're completely natural, always made fresh and packed with healing roots, leaves and rhizomes. In Bali, it's widely acknowledged that food is medicine, and it's not uncommon for people to tailor their diets to their constitution, spiritual beliefs and even their temperament. This goes beyond the realm of spices into plants and animals and their various characteristics, traits and meanings. Ducks and geese, for example, are selective natural foragers and are considered fine, clean proteins. Sea turtles, too, were once considered refined meat. Pineapple is not for the hot-headed, as it generates heat in the body, while cucumber is known to be cooling. Rice is believed to have been bestowed upon us directly from the heavens – the perfect food. The cow is sacred and represents the mother; it rarely features on the Balinese menu.

In short, the connection between what we eat and who we are is intrinsic and shapes the way we consume. There are ancient philosophies that expand on this in detail, but put very simply, it comes down to this: you are what you eat, so eat wisely.

Makes 700 g (1 lb 9 oz)

- 2 teaspoons freshly grated nutmeg
- 8 cloves
- 6 long black peppercorns, or ½ teaspoon ground black pepper
- 1½ tablespoons shrimp paste
- 120 ml (4 fl oz/½ cup) coconut oil (for a recipe, see page 97)
- 10 salam leaves
- sea salt and pepper

SPICE MIX
- 275 g (9½ oz/approx. 12) red (Asian) shallots
- 150 g (5½ oz/approx. 30) garlic cloves
- 4 long red chillies, seeds removed
- 50 g (1¾ oz/approx. 18) tabasco chillies
- 40 g (1½ oz/approx. 18 cm/ 7 in piece) fresh turmeric
- 2 cm (¾ in) piece fresh ginger
- 45 g (1½ oz/¼ cup/approx. 18 cm/7 in piece) freshly grated lesser galangal
- 6 cm (2½ in) piece fresh galangal
- 2 lemongrass stems, white part only

Out of all the recipes in this book this is probably the most important. Let's rephrase that – it is the most important. Base genep, or base gede, is the backbone of Balinese cooking. It lends its complexity, punch and turmeric tinge to most of the island's meat-based dishes – ceremonial sates, homemade stews and grilled delicacies alike. Its name is a testament to its blockbuster list of ingredients and uses – base means spice, genep means complete and gede means large. All Balinese cooks have their own take on base genep, and many adjust the quantities of each ingredient to suit the dish they're cooking. We've created a formula that works nicely across all the recipes in this book, but feel free to experiment to suit your taste.

BASE GENEP
THE ESSENTIAL SPICE PASTE

To make the spice mix, roughly chop all the ingredients. Using a mortar and pestle, pound everything together until it forms a rough paste. Transfer the mixture to a bowl and set aside.

In the mortar and pestle, crush the nutmeg, cloves and peppercorns into a coarse powder.

Toast the shrimp paste in a wok or frying pan over a low heat until it is aromatic, about 1 minute.

Heat the oil in a medium saucepan over a high heat. Add the shrimp paste and spice mix and cook for 3–4 minutes, stirring continuously to make sure nothing sticks or burns. When all the liquid has evaporated and a dark green paste has formed, add the dry spices and salam leaves and give it another stir.

Turn the heat down, cover and let it simmer for 3 hours, stirring gently every 10–15 minutes.

When the paste is ready, it will be smooth and aromatic. Season with salt and pepper to taste. Set aside to cool. Store in an airtight container in the fridge for up to 2 weeks.

Makes 1.6 kg (3½ lb)

— 200 ml (7 fl oz) coconut oil
  (for a recipe, see page 97)
— 600 ml (20½ fl oz) water
— 2 tablespoons shrimp paste
— 70 g (2½ oz / ⅓ cup) palm
  sugar, shaved or finely
  grated
— 1½ tablespoons sea salt

SPICE MIX
— 500 g (1 lb 2 oz / approx. 20)
  red (Asian) shallots
— 250 g (9 oz / approx. 50)
  garlic cloves
— 130 g (4½ oz) fresh galangal
— 70 g (2½ oz) fresh turmeric
— 6 cm (2½ in) piece fresh
  ginger
— 60 g (2 oz / ¼ cup firmly
  packed) freshly grated lesser
  galangal
— 90 g (3 oz / approx. 30)
  tabasco chillies
— 10 lemongrass stems,
  white part only
— 10 candlenuts, roasted
  (see page 26)
— 2 tablespoons whole white
  peppercorns, toasted
  (see page 28)
— 2 tablespoons whole black
  peppercorns, toasted
  (see page 28)
— 2 tablespoons cloves
— 2 tablespoons freshly grated
  nutmeg

This chopped base is used to season ceremonial foods such as lawar (see page 240) and the Balinese pork sausages known as Urutan (page 254). It's a combination of quite a lot of roots and aromatics, which makes it earthy, complex and powerful. In short, it's a big-flavoured spice mix. Traditionally, the ingredients are finely chopped using a heavy-bladed cleaver called a belakas. More than a cooking technique, chopping is a spiritual practice of sorts that's deeply rhythmic, meditative and plays a big role in a range of food-based rituals.

If you decide to try the traditional method, use the heaviest-bladed knife or cleaver you can find. Bring the ingredients together as you chop them, using the blade to sweep or fold them towards the centre of the chopping board. When it is ready, it'll resemble a very fine salsa – you almost want it to look and feel like sand. You could use a food processor or meat grinder to save time; just be mindful not to over-process the spices into a paste.

BASE RAJANG

CHOPPED SPICES

To make the spice mix, roughly chop all the ingredients individually, then finely chop them together to combine them. Place in a large bowl and set aside.

Heat the oil in a saucepan over a high heat until it reaches smoke point. Add the spice mix and cook, stirring continuously, for about 5 minutes.

Reduce the heat to low and continue cooking for about 1–2 hours, stirring every 10–15 minutes and gradually adding the water to prevent the mixture from sticking and burning.

Meanwhile, toast the shrimp paste in a wok or frying pan over a low heat until it is aromatic, about 1 minute. Set aside until needed.

Add the sugar, shrimp paste and salt to the base and give it another stir. You'll know it's ready when it's almost dark green in colour and releases an earthy fragrance. Set aside to cool. Store in an airtight container in the fridge for up to 3 weeks.

Makes 250 g (9 oz)

- 2½ tablespoons freshly grated nutmeg
- 1 teaspoon cloves
- ½ teaspoon ground cumin
- 1 tablespoon whole coriander seeds
- 5 long black peppercorns
- ½ teaspoon whole white peppercorns
- 2½ cm (1 in) sweet rush (see page 129, optional)
- 125 g (4½ oz/approx. 25) garlic cloves, sliced
- 2 cm (¾ in) piece fresh ginger, sliced
- 2½ tablespoons (approx. 25 g/1 oz) finely chopped fresh lesser galangal
- 5 cm (2 in) piece fresh galangal, sliced
- 3–4 candlenuts, roasted (see page 26)
- 150 ml (5 fl oz) coconut oil (for a recipe, see page 97)
- 1 teaspoon shrimp paste
- sea salt

This aromatic spice paste is used to bring complexity and medicinal undertones to the glassy pork stew known as Balung (page 246). Up in the mountains of Kintamani in central Bali, it's used to brighten the muddiness of lake-caught tilapia in a dish known as mujair nyat-nyat. If you prefer a peppery heat over the spicy heat of chillies, it's a wonderful spice paste to have on hand. Morning market vendors often sell portioned packages of nutmeg, cloves, peppercorns, coriander seeds and candlenuts ready to be ground and combined with the fresh ingredients at home.

BASE WANGEN
AROMATIC SPICE PASTE

Toast the whole dry spices over a medium heat for 2–3 minutes. Stir continuously to prevent them from burning.

Grind the spices into a powder using a mortar and pestle or a spice grinder. Set aside.

Using a mortar and pestle, crush the sweet rush, if using, garlic, ginger, galangals and candlenuts into a paste.

Heat the oil in a medium saucepan over a high heat until it reaches smoke point. Add the spice paste and sauté for 2 minutes, or until fragrant.

Reduce the heat to low and add the powdered spices and shrimp paste. Cook for 1–1½ hours, stirring occasionally to help the sugars release without burning. The goal is to caramelise the spices, so you'll know the paste is done when the raw ingredients release a sweet, earthy aroma and the base is dark brown. Season to taste with salt. Store in an airtight container in the fridge for 2–3 weeks.

Makes 450 g (1 lb)

- 15 cm (6 in) piece fresh turmeric, roughly chopped
- 115 g (4 oz/¾ cup) roughly chopped fresh lesser galangal
- 1 cm (½ in) piece fresh ginger, roughly chopped
- 115 g (4 oz/approx. 30) garlic cloves, roughly chopped
- 1 red (Asian) shallot, roughly chopped
- 3 candlenuts, roasted (see page 26), roughly chopped
- 9 tabasco chillies, roughly chopped
- 100 ml (3½ fl oz) coconut oil (for a recipe, see page 97)
- 250 ml (8½ fl oz/1 cup) water
- 2 teaspoons sea salt
- 1 teaspoon sugar

This is basically Suna cekuh (page 56) with the addition of turmeric. It's often used as a seasoning for poultry and seafood dishes such as Pepes be pasih (page 187).

BASE KUNING
YELLOW SPICE PASTE

Using a large mortar and pestle, crush the turmeric, lesser galangal, ginger, garlic, shallot, candlenuts and chillies into a paste.

Heat the oil in a wok over a high heat until it reaches smoke point. Turn the heat down to medium, add the spice paste and slowly stir in the water over 2 minutes.

Reduce the heat to low and continue cooking the paste for 45 minutes–1 hour, or until all the liquid has evaporated and it forms a deep-yellow paste.

Add the salt and sugar, give it a good stir and cook over a low heat for a further 10 minutes. Adjust the seasoning to taste. It's ready when it's dark yellow in colour with a bright aroma and a punchy, earthy flavour. Store in an airtight container in the fridge for 2–3 weeks.

Makes 500 g (1 lb 2 oz)

— 8 candlenuts, roasted
  (see page 26)
— 210 g (7½ oz/approx. 40)
  garlic cloves, crushed
  (see page 28)
— 125 g (4½ oz/1 cup) finely
  chopped fresh lesser galangal
— 1 teaspoon salt
— 100 ml (3½ fl oz) coconut oil
  (for a recipe, see page 97)
— 400 ml (13½ fl oz/1⅔ cups)
  water

'This is a quick and simple base for vegetable dishes, grilled seafood and stir-fries – a natural MSG, if you like. My earliest memory of suna cekuh is when I was a kid living on Nusa Penida, where my mother would make baby octopus slathered in this spice paste with slivers of chilli for heat. To this day, it's still one of my favourite Balinese flavours and it always reminds me of home.'
  – *Wayan*

SUNA CEKUH

GARLIC AND LESSER GALANGAL SEASONING

Using a mortar and pestle, crush the candlenuts, garlic, lesser galangal and salt into a paste.

Heat the oil in a medium saucepan over a medium heat. Add the spice paste and cook for 3 minutes, stirring continuously.

Reduce the heat to low, add 100 ml (3½ fl oz) of the water and cook for 45 minutes, stirring occasionally and adding more water gradually to prevent it from sticking to the bottom or burning. The paste is ready when it is soft, evenly caramelised with a light brown colour and has a sweet, earthy aroma. Set aside to cool. Keep in an airtight container in the fridge for up to 2 weeks.

Makes 650 g (1 lb 7 oz)

- 14 cm (5½ in) piece fresh
  ginger, roughly chopped
- 300 g (10½ oz/approx. 14)
  red (Asian) shallots,
  roughly chopped
- 100 g (3½ oz/approx. 20)
  garlic cloves, roughly
  chopped
- 6 cm (2½ in) piece fresh
  galangal, roughly chopped
- 1 tablespoon finely chopped
  fresh lesser galangal
- 80 g (2¾ oz) fresh turmeric,
  roughly chopped
- 1 cm (½ in) cassumunar
  ginger (see page 274),
  roughly chopped (optional)
- 40 g (1½ oz/approx. 16–20)
  tabasco chillies
- 10 long red chillies
  (see page 274)
- 150 ml (5 fl oz) coconut oil
  (for a recipe, see page 97)
- 2 teaspoons ground white
  pepper
- 2 teaspoons shrimp paste
- 5 salam leaves
- 1 tablespoon sea salt
- 250 ml (8½ fl oz/1 cup)
  water

A powerful paste from north Bali that pairs well with seafood. Use it in Jero Yudi's ikan bungbung (page 196).

BASE BAWANG JAHE
SHALLOT, GARLIC AND GINGER PASTE

Using a mortar and pestle, grind the ginger, shallot, garlic, galangals, turmeric, cassumunar ginger, if using, and chillies into a chunky paste.

Heat the oil in a medium saucepan over a medium heat until it reaches smoke point. Add the spice paste and cook for 5 minutes, stirring continuously, until fragrant.

Add 100 ml (3½ fl oz) of the water, the pepper, shrimp paste, salam leaves and sea salt. Reduce the heat to low and cook for 1 hour, stirring every 15 minutes and adding more water gradually to prevent it sticking to the bottom and burning. It will be dark yellow and fragrant when it's ready.

Remove the pan from the heat, stir it once more and let it cool in the pan at room temperature. Once cooled, you can store it in an airtight container in the fridge for up to 3 weeks.

CLANS AND CLIMATES

A JOURNEY FROM THE SEA TO THE MOUNTAINS

Wayan and I are heading along the rugged Buleleng coastline to a village called Les to dig a little deeper into the food of Bali's north. Compared to, say, Sumatera, Java or Borneo, Bali is a remarkably small island – just 153 km (95 miles) wide and 112 km (70 miles) from top to bottom – yet, from a cultural, geographical and culinary standpoint, it's a marvel – a patchwork, if you like, of states, clans and former kingdoms, each with their own histories, customs and flavours.

These days, the culinary lines between the different regions have blurred. We now have multi-chain supermarkets, trucks that transport animals from large-scale farms from one regency to the next, and vegetables that are imported from neighbouring islands and countries. You can find hot Gilimanuk-style betutu (spiced, smoked poultry) and jaja (traditional cakes or sweets) from Gianyar in parts of Denpasar and wider Badung, and a lot of the traditional cooking methods – steaming, grilling and smoking – have been replaced with deep-frying. In many cases, store-bought vegetable oil is used instead of homemade coconut oil, and coconut milk from cans or cartons is used in place of the hand-squeezed fresh stuff. But a good number of people remain dedicated to preserving regional and traditional cooking techniques and ingredients – my niang (grandmother), for example, who claims that food is part of our budaya (culture) and keeps us in touch with who we are.

The people of Les are part of a community known as Bali Mula – a clan whose belief systems and practices predate those of the island's majority Javanese–Hindu descendant population. Some of the original Balinese, if you like. We leave Ubud just before noon, taking the longer route, which cuts through the leafy rice-growing villages of Bongkasa and Punggul, then winds up into the vegetable-farming highlands of Bedugul, where the cooler climate favours the likes of cabbage, carrots, lettuce and strawberries – foods introduced to appease the masses. The forests and farms along the way are lush and well watered. It's the end of the rainy season, and fruit stalls are stationed along the quiet country roads, stacked high with red, ripe rambutans, seasonal butter avocadoes, jackfruits the size and weight of a small child, and dangerous-looking and pungent durians.

As we descend into the region's capital, Singaraja, the landscape changes — and so does the food. The narrow streets are lined with European-accented shops and houses that speak to the city's colonial past. They rub shoulders with ornate mosques, Chinese temples and several eateries offering sio bak roast pork and lapciong sausages — legacies left by the sailors who traded here for centuries. But as fascinating as Peranakan food is, we keep driving. Our sights are set on a kitchen about an hour from here, where we're slated to meet chef and local priest Jero Mangku Dalem Suci Gede Yudiawan.

We arrive at his place by nightfall and the open-air dining room is softly lit. Rows of antique clay pots rest against the woven bamboo walls; they're housing arak (traditional palm wine) that is ageing and infusing with the likes of fresh mango, jackfruit and moringa leaves. There's a little bar dedicated to the spirit on our left, and a wooden bridge to our right that leads to the paon. One of the cooks, a young man no older than twenty-five with an impressive tattoo sleeve down his right arm, tells us Jero Yudiawan is officiating a ceremony and will be here shortly. He invites us to explore the kitchen while we wait. It's set in a small, open structure with work benches on either side and a neat earthen stove in its centre. Jero Yudiawan's knives are proudly displayed along the back wall; there's more than ten, most of them cleavers, a couple of them serrated for cutting through fish bones. An elevated bale pavilion where the mise en place happens sits adjacent to the hearth. A huge volcanic-stone ulekan (mortar), an even larger tamarind-wood talenan (chopping board) and glass jars full of spices, roots and aromatics are spread across the wooden boards. Two fat roosters rest surprisingly calmly underneath all the chopping and pounding.

Jero Yudiawan arrives dressed in his immaculate all-white ceremonial attire. He excuses himself momentarily and returns in a more laid-back version of the previous outfit — a white kamben (sarong) and t-shirt, his headcloth removed and hair pulled back in a low bun. He and Wayan bond instantly over the similarities of coastline cooking in the north and on Nusa Penida. 'Heat and spice,' Jero Yudiawan says, 'that's what characterises our food.'

The northern climate, he tells us, is harsh and dry. They eat seafood, mainly, with papaya, cassava and Javanese long pepper leaves for vegetables. Before rice was widely accessible, they'd make nasi sela (cassava root 'rice') similar to the dried and grated cassava of Wayan's home island. If times were bountiful, they might stir some actual beras (uncooked rice) into the mix.

Top left: Jero Mangku Dalem Suci Gede Yudiawan in his kitchen.
Top right: Lontar palm fruits.
Bottom left: Arak at the end of the distillation process at Dapur Bali Mula.
Bottom right: Cloves drying in the sun just outside of Singaraja, north Bali.

Left: Mount Batur, Mount Abang and Mount Agung as seen from Kintamani.

The sea up north is wild and deep, so squid, octopus, lobster and deep-sea fish are the prime sources of protein. Jero Yudiawan serves us mackerel three ways – diced and tossed with a red sambal, simmered low-and-slow in a spicy fish head soup, and cooked in a tube of young bamboo with yellow spices and turmeric leaves in a dish he calls Ikan bungbung (page 196). Dessert is Daluman leaf jelly (page 266) with homemade coconut milk and juruh – a type of lontar palm sugar that resembles honey in its colour and thickness. It's smoky, complex and almost savoury on the tongue. We cap off the evening with six shots of arak, made from lontar nectar, which Jero Yudiawan produces the old-fashioned way using a wood fire, no yeasts, and long bamboo poles that cool the clear liquor before it trickles into glass bottles at the end of the production line. As we imbibe, we talk about the state of traditional cooking in Bali. 'This kind of food is almost gone,' he says. 'I've had chefs work for me who can't make sambal but can cook spaghetti with their eyes closed. I want to make and preserve the kind of food that people miss.'

From the hot, dry north-east, we pay a visit to the mountains to visit Kentri Norberg, the proprietor of a biodynamic coffee estate and retreat at the base of Mount Batukaru. The central peaks of Bali – the Batukaru range towards the west, Mount Agung out east and the Kintamani caldera in between them – are the island's most impressive landmarks. They are laced with freshwater springs, high-altitude farms and tegals (forests) teeming with traditional foods (see page 125). Water is delicately manoeuvred from the holy lakes of the highlands towards the lowland rice fields via a series of channels and streams known as the subak. And so, the mountains are the origins of the island's fertility and are revered and protected by both the people and spirits that reside on and around their slopes.

'The energies here are strong,' says Ibu Kentri, as she's affectionately known, 'particularly over near the yoga shala (yoga studio or pavilion). That's why we've never built rooms up there.'

She spent most of her childhood there, darting between her family's garden, the local primary school and the temple across the road where her father was a priest and caretaker. At Batukaru Coffee Estate, she cooks the kind of food she ate growing up: 'highly nutritious, not overly processed, how the village used to cook.'

In the open-air dining pavilion, Ibu Kentri is telling us about jaka trees. From the pavilion looking out over the island's south and east, with glimpses of the western coastline to our right, almost all of the surrounding mountains are visible, except for Batukaru behind us and Mount Agung, which is concealed behind rain clouds. Ibu Kentri points to a group of tall, fat jaka palms: 'We sweeten our coffee with juruh sugar made from these palms. There's only one old man in the village who still produces this kind of sugar. When he's gone it won't exist here anymore.'

Ibu Kentri's estate sprawls across 10 hectares of jungle and coffee trees. From the cool, wild land, she cultivates and forages a number of local plants – young bamboo, moringa leaves, cassava leaves and roots, kara beans and sembung (ngai camphor) among them – which she serves with fluffy mansur rice that grows in the heritage fields below. She serves us a pot of homegrown bamboo shoots in a bright yellow broth, and freshly foraged young fern tips sautéed with garlic, red (Asian) shallots and chillies, with just the right amount of kuah (juice) to pour over our rice. She deep-fries the rest of the fern tips in a turmeric-spiked batter with a side of sambal fragrant with torch ginger stems. She smiles as we reach for second helpings, commenting on how everything tastes so alive. 'This place, these foods can cure many things.'

Nearby, in the village of Belulang, we visit a temple called Pura Luhur Batu Panes. Today happens to be an auspicious day, Kajeng Kliwon, when the spirits and other elemental forces are believed to be potent, present and active across the three worlds. In an effort to neutralise or tap into this energy, Hindu devotees dive into ritual – purifying inside and out, laying out specific offerings and asking the energy of Siwa for protection from any negativity that might be floating around in the ether. At this particular event, a new pratima (idol) is being planted in one of the temple shrines. The rituals are conducted first, followed by prayers and, after that, we are invited to eat.

Left: Kentri Norberg among the coffee trees of Batukaru Coffee Estate.
Top left: Grinding corn for fritters.

Pura Luhur Batu Panes is unique in that it's vast and wall-less. Forest provides the backdrop for the pelinggih shrines, and rice-terraces hug the rest of the complex gently between their dips and curves. The kitchen backs onto brilliant vistas of newly planted rice fields and dormant mountains slumbering peacefully underneath a mess of grey clouds. From these regions emerge large tubs of steaming white rice, smoky chicken and banana trunk wrapped and steamed in cacao leaves, and a kind of sweet coconut floss known as sambal nyuh – a speciality of the region. Instead of cakes, we're offered roasted yams and bananas, served plain and simple with a cup of sweet coffee. The woman next to me giggles as she peels the skin from her banana. 'This is how we eat,' she says, 'do you like it?'

Left: The rice fields of Belulang, Tabanan.
Top left: Freshly foraged fern tips.
Top right: Kentri Norberg preparing lunch at Batukaru Coffee Estate.

Makes 500 ml (17 fl oz/2 cups)

— 12½ cm (5 in) piece fresh
  turmeric, roughly chopped
— 500 ml (17 fl oz/2 cups)
  filtered water

This recipe acts like a marinade. In the days before refrigeration, turmeric was used as an antibacterial agent that also helped remove any unpleasant smells from meat and seafood, and many older cooks still practise this today. Always use fresh turmeric for this recipe, and if you're using the traditional hand-pressed method, be mindful that you might have faintly yellow fingers for a few days.

AIR KUNYIT
TURMERIC WATER

Blend the turmeric and water in a blender or food processor on high speed for 2 minutes, or until it's nice and smooth. Strain. This will keep in an airtight container in the fridge for up to 3 days.

TRADITIONAL METHOD

The old-school way to do this is to grate the turmeric using a pangikihan (page 38) or microplane and then to squeeze it through the water with your hand until the two liquids are well combined before straining.

Makes 250 g (9 oz)

- 200 g (7 oz / 1 cup) shrimp paste
- 2½ tablespoons sea salt
- 100 ml (3½ fl oz) coconut oil (for a recipe, see page 97)

There's nothing quite like the smell of terasi (shrimp paste) toasting in the morning – or the smell of terasi at all, for that matter. Rich, intense and pungent, this salty shrimp paste is one of the most powerful seasonings in the paon. It weaves its way into chopped dishes such as lawar (see page 240) and urab (see page 132), sambals and spice pastes, more often than not in the form of this three-ingredient flavour bomb: uyah sere.

Toasting refines the flavour of terasi, while the sea salt and coconut oil help it soften and break down so that it incorporates more evenly into the dish. Most cooks adjust the ratio to suit their liking, so don't be afraid to experiment and add or subtract the amount of terasi you use, depending on how much extra flavour you want to bring to your cooking.

UYAH SERE

SALTY SHRIMP PASTE SEASONING

Heat a medium saucepan over a low heat for 3 minutes. Fry the shrimp paste on one side for about 2 minutes, or until it releases a pungent aroma, then cook the other side for 2 minutes. Take off the heat and let it cool at room temperature for about 10 minutes.

Once cooled, place on a chopping board. Slice it using a heavy-bladed knife while combining it with the salt as you chop, working the two ingredients together for about 4 minutes until they reach a paste-like consistency. You can use your fingers to massage out any large chunks, but be aware that they will smell quite strongly of fermented shrimp for a while afterwards.

Heat the oil in a wok or medium saucepan over a medium heat until it reaches smoke point. Add the paste and sauté for 2–3 minutes.

The paste will keep in a glass jar at room temperature for 1 week, or in the fridge for up to 2 months.

Makes 2 litres (68 fl oz/8 cups)

- 100 ml (3½ fl oz) vegetable oil
- 2 onions, cut into 1 cm (½ in) cubes
- 3 carrots, cut into 1 cm (½ in) cubes
- 5 celery stalks, cut into 1 cm (½ in) pieces
- 2 garlic bulbs, cut in half horizontally
- 2½ teaspoons whole black peppercorns, lightly toasted (see page 28)
- 7 salam leaves
- 2.5 litres (85 fl oz/10 cups) water

Stocks are not classically Balinese, but they can be used to elevate a number of the recipes in this book. For stews and soups, just replace the water in the ingredients list with stock to make it extra gurih (tasty).

KALDU SAYUR
VEGETABLE STOCK

Heat the oil in a large stockpot over a high heat. Add the onion, carrot, celery, garlic, peppercorns and salam leaves, and sweat, stirring constantly to prevent burning or sticking to the pot, for about 8 minutes, or until the vegetables have softened.

Add the water and bring to the boil.

Turn the heat down to low and simmer, uncovered, for about 2 hours.

Strain the stock into a large mixing bowl, discarding the vegetables.

Place the bowl inside a larger casserole dish or pan filled with ice water (this step allows the vegetable stock to cool quickly for immediate use or storage). The stock will keep in the fridge for up to 1 week, or for up to 6 months in the freezer.

Makes 1.5 litres (51 fl oz/6 cups)

- 1 kg (2 lb 3 oz) fish bones, preferably snapper
- 2 litres (68 fl oz/8 cups) water
- 1 small onion, diced
- 10 garlic cloves, crushed (see page 28)
- 1 leek, thickly sliced
- 3 celery stalks, thickly sliced
- 1 lemongrass stem, green and white parts, crushed (see page 28)

A simple fish stock that brings extra depth to seafood dishes.

KALDU IKAN
FISH STOCK

Rinse the fish bones under hot running water to clean off any excess blood.

Place all the ingredients in a large stockpot and bring to the boil over a high heat. Reduce the heat to low and let it simmer for about 2 hours.

Strain the stock into a mixing bowl, discarding the bones and vegetables.

Place the bowl inside a larger casserole dish or pan filled with ice water (this step allows the stock to cool quickly for immediate use or storage). The stock will keep in the fridge for up to 1 week, or for up to 6 months in the freezer.

- 3 kg (6 lb 10 oz) chicken bones
- 6 cm (2½ in) piece fresh ginger, unpeeled
- 1 large carrot, cut into 1 cm (½ in) cubes
- 1 large onion, cut into 1 cm (½ in) cubes
- 2 celery stalks, cut into 1 cm (½ in) pieces
- 1 tablespoon whole coriander seeds, toasted (see page 28)
- 1 tablespoon whole black peppercorns, toasted (see page 28)
- 2 lemongrass stems, green and white parts, crushed and knotted (see page 28)
- 1 garlic bulb, cut in half horizontally
- 5 litres (170 fl oz/20 cups) water

This chicken stock is loaded with roots and spices, giving it a rich, earthy flavour that works well in Balinese cooking. Use it to bring flavour to Jukut nangka (page 151), Serosop (page 201) and any other soup or stew.

KALDU AYAM

CHICKEN STOCK

Preheat the oven to 185°C (365°F).

Place the bones on a baking tray and roast them in the oven for 1 hour.

Meanwhile, roast the ginger over an open flame until partially charred. Alternatively, you can roast the ginger on a tray in the oven at 200°C (400°F), or under the oven grill (broiler) for 10 minutes. Smash the roasted ginger, skin and all, with the back of a knife and set it aside.

Place the roasted bones in a large stockpot along with all the other ingredients, making sure everything is submerged in the water, and bring to the boil over a high heat.

Turn the heat down to low and simmer for 6–10 hours, skimming off any impurities that rise to the surface. The longer it simmers the more intense the flavours will be, so taste it as you go.

Once you're happy with the potency of the stock, strain it, discarding the bones, vegetables and spices, and set it aside to cool. The stock will keep in an airtight container in the fridge for up to 5 days, or in the freezer for up to 6 months.

Makes 200 g (7 oz)

— 10 garlic cloves, sliced
— 200 g (7 oz / approx. 36)
  tabasco chillies, sliced
— sea salt

FRIED SHALLOTS
Makes 20 g / ¾ oz
— 100 ml (3½ fl oz) coconut oil
  (for a recipe, see page 97)
— 3 red (Asian) shallots, sliced

This is a fried sambal that's often served as a condiment or tossed through a dish as a finishing element. Most people make it fresh every day. It's hot, punchy and sweet from the golden-brown, caramelised fried shallots, garlic and chillies, all slightly crisped around the edges but still juicy on the inside. Sambal goreng has an incredible umami quality that'll make you want to serve it with everything. We personally like it with Urab kacang (page 134), Jukut nangka (page 151) and most poultry dishes.

SAMBAL GORENG
DEEP-FRIED SAMBAL

To make the fried shallots, heat the oil in a wok over a high heat. Add the shallots, reduce the heat to medium and sauté until they have golden crisp edges and soft centres. Remove the shallots from the pan with a spider ladle or slotted spoon and set aside on a plate lined with paper towel.

Add the garlic to the wok and fry over a medium heat for 5–8 minutes, or until golden. Take care not to burn the garlic or it will turn bitter. Set aside with the shallots.

Add the chillies and cook for about 5 minutes, or until they're wilted. Don't let them crisp up – they should be juicy on the inside. Remove them using a spider ladle or slotted spoon and transfer to a medium mixing bowl.

Add the fried shallots and garlic to the bowl with the chilli and toss until well combined. Season with salt to taste.

This is best used fresh, but it can be stored in a covered bowl at room temperature for one day (no longer) if needed.

- 150 g (5½ oz/approx. 6) red
  (Asian) shallots, finely sliced
- 18 tabasco chillies, finely
  sliced
- 4 lemongrass stems, white
  part only, finely sliced
- 6 lime leaves, finely chopped
- 80 ml (2½ fl oz/⅓ cup)
  coconut oil (for a recipe,
  see page 97)
- 1 tablespoon lime juice
- 2 teaspoons shrimp paste,
  lightly fried
- sea salt, to taste

'This sambal is similar to a salsa. It's probably Bali's best-loved condiment and every region, village and household adds their own twists to it. Shallots, chillies, sea salt and coconut oil are the foundations. Some cooks add torch ginger flower, garlic or chopped ginger. I like to use lemongrass for its aroma. Once you've mastered sambal matah, you can use it to elevate grilled seafood and chicken, or even plain rice. Slice the ingredients as finely as possible and use your fingers to do the mixing.'
– Wayan

WAYAN'S SAMBAL MATAH
RAW SAMBAL WITH LEMONGRASS

Using your hands, toss the shallot, chilli, lemongrass and lime leaves together in a medium mixing bowl.

Heat the coconut oil in a small saucepan over a medium heat for 3–4 minutes and pour it into the mixing bowl.

Let the mixture cool slightly, and, using your hands, gently squeeze everything together to incorporate the coconut oil into the other ingredients.

Add the lime juice and shrimp paste and toss again. Season with salt to taste and you're ready to go. Sambal matah is best eaten fresh, so we don't recommend storing it.

Makes 150 g (5½ oz)

- 250 ml (8½ fl oz/1 cup) coconut oil (for a recipe, see page 97)
- 250 g (9 oz) red (Asian) shallots, sliced
- 160 g (5½ oz/approx. 35) garlic cloves, finely sliced
- 40 (100 g/3½ oz) tabasco chillies, finely sliced
- 10 lime leaves, finely sliced
- 1 tablespoon lime juice
- salt and pepper

Mbe (pronounced em-burr) is a sweet, hot and smoky sambal that can make something as simple as a bowl of plain steamed rice shine. We dare you not to eat the whole batch in one go.

SAMBAL MBE

SHALLOT AND GARLIC SAMBAL

Heat the oil in a small frying pan or wok over a medium heat. Add the shallots and fry until golden-brown and crisp but not burnt.

Remove the shallots from the pan and lay them on a tray lined with paper towel to remove any excess oil.

Strain the oil and pour it back into the wok or pan. Heat the oil over a medium heat, add the garlic and fry for 2–3 minutes, or until golden and crisp around the edges. Remove the garlic using a spider ladle or slotted spoon and place on the paper towel with the shallots.

Strain the oil again and repeat the same method with the chillies, frying them until just wilted but not crisp, then place them in a medium mixing bowl.

Add the fried shallot, garlic, lime leaves and lime juice to the bowl with the chillies and season to taste with salt and pepper. This is best eaten the day it's made, but it can be kept in an airtight container in the fridge for up to 3 days.

Makes 200 g (7 oz)

— 10–12 small red (Asian)
  shallots, finely sliced
— 3 garlic cloves, finely sliced
— 2 small green bird's eye
  chillies (see page 274),
  finely sliced
— 3 small red bird's eye chillies
  (see page 274), finely sliced
— thin slice of fresh ginger,
  crushed (see page 28) and
  finely chopped
— 2 lime leaves, finely sliced
— 2 tablespoons coconut oil
  (for a recipe, see page 97)
— sea salt, to taste (I add about
  1 teaspoon)
— ½ lime, to serve

'Whenever I came home from Australia, my niang (grandmother) would make her sambal matah, and I would inspect it intensely to try and figure out what made it so delicious. There was something hidden in among the chillies and shallots. It wasn't lemongrass or terasi (shrimp paste), and it certainly wasn't MSG. For a long time, I was stumped. One day she finally revealed the secret to her formula. "It's ginger," she said. "Not too much and chopped very finely so that it doesn't overpower the shallots and garlic." Here's my niang's recipe, which pairs particularly well with chicken – although I dollop it over pretty much anything that's savoury.'

— *Maya*

NIANG'S SAMBAL MATAH

RAW SAMBAL WITH GINGER

Add the shallot, garlic, chilli, ginger and lime leaves to a small mixing bowl and toss together using your hands. Slowly pour in the oil and season with salt to taste. The consistency should be wet but not swimming in oil. In other words, you want it to be lubricated and lifted by the flavour of the coconut oil, but not runny.

Squeeze the lime over the top and serve. This is best eaten fresh.

Tip

For more fragrance and pungency, you can add finely sliced torch ginger flower or a tiny sliver of terasi (shrimp paste), no more than the size of a peanut, making sure you massage it through the sambal well using your fingers.

Makes approx. 300 g (10½ oz)

— 1 large roma (plum) tomato,
  seeds removed and roughly
  sliced
— 1 small torch ginger flower
  stem, finely sliced
— 1 long red chilli (see page
  274; we like Fresno chillies
  for this recipe), seeds
  removed and sliced
— 6 tabasco chillies, sliced
— 1 red (Asian) shallot, sliced
— 4 garlic cloves, sliced
— 80 ml (2½ fl oz / ⅓ cup)
  coconut oil (for a recipe,
  see page 97)
— ¼ teaspoon shrimp paste,
  rolled into a small ball
— sea salt, to taste
— 1 tablespoon palm sugar

Bongkot is what we call the stems of the torch ginger flower. They have a really interesting flavour profile – rich, highly perfumed and slightly savoury – making them a great addition to sauces and sambals. This sambal pairs nicely with poultry and seafood.

SAMBAL ULEK BONGKOT
TORCH GINGER FLOWER SAMBAL

Using a mortar and pestle, crush the tomato into a chunky purée and set it aside in a small bowl. Next, grind the torch ginger flower, chillies, shallot and garlic into a rough paste and set aside in a separate bowl.

Heat the oil in a medium saucepan or wok over a medium heat. Add the chilli paste and sauté for 3–4 minutes.

Add the tomato purée, reduce the heat to low and continue cooking for about 1 hour, stirring occasionally to prevent it from burning.

When the sambal is dark red and caramelised with a sweet, gentle heat and no raw flavours, add the shrimp paste, salt and sugar and stir well. Taste and adjust the seasoning if needed.

Take off the heat and let it cool on the counter before storing or serving. It'll keep in a glass jar or airtight container in the fridge for up to 2 weeks.

Makes 350 g (12½ oz)

— bamboo steamer
— toothpicks
— 20 × 100 cm (8 × 40 in)
   banana leaf or equivalent
   parchment paper

— 9 long red chillies (see
   page 274), seeds removed
— 8 tabasco chillies, seeds
   removed
— 5 red (Asian) shallots
— 10 garlic cloves
— 2½ tablespoons coconut oil
   (for a recipe, see page 97)
— 1½ tablespoons shrimp paste
— 1 teaspoon lime juice
— large pinch of sea salt

A light, chunky, medium-heat sambal that is popular in and around Ubud and the wider Gianyar area. The lime juice gives it a gentle tang that pairs beautifully with poultry.

SAMBAL KUKUS
STEAMED SAMBAL

Combine the chillies, shallot and garlic in a mixing bowl, then wrap the mixture in a piece of banana leaf (see page 27 for a guide) or parchment paper, closing it with toothpicks.

Place a bamboo steamer over a pot of boiling water over a medium heat. Place the packet in the steamer, cover and steam for about 10 minutes, or until all the ingredients have softened.

Remove the packet from the steamer and set aside to cool for about 10 minutes, or until cool enough to handle.

Meanwhile, heat the coconut oil in a small saucepan over a low heat for about 3 minutes and set aside.

Remove the ingredients from the packet and crush them into a chunky paste using a mortar and pestle. Add the shrimp paste, lime juice, salt and warm coconut oil, and continue crushing the mixture until everything is well combined. Serve fresh.

Makes 250 g (9 oz)

- 3 roma (plum) tomatoes, seeds removed, sliced
- 100 ml (3½ fl oz) water
- 4 red (Asian) shallots, roughly chopped
- 6 garlic cloves, sliced
- 1 Fresno chilli, seeds removed, sliced
- 9 tabasco chillies, sliced
- 100 ml (3½ fl oz) coconut oil (for a recipe, see page 97)
- 1½ tablespoons sea salt
- 2 tablespoons sugar
- ¼ teaspoon shrimp paste (optional)

This sambal is a wonderful companion for everything from rice to stir-fried greens to grilled meats. The shrimp paste adds quite a bit of punch, but you can leave it out for a less intense result. It should taste sweet and tangy from the tomatoes with a gentle heat from the chillies.

SAMBAL TOMAT

TOMATO SAMBAL

Using a mortar and pestle, crush the tomatoes and water into a chunky puree. Pour the mixture into a medium bowl and set aside. Next, crush the shallots, garlic and chillies. Set aside.

Heat the oil in a large saucepan or wok over a high heat for 3 minutes, or until it reaches smoke point. Add the chilli paste and cook for 4–5 minutes, stirring continuously.

Add the tomato paste, turn the heat down to low and simmer for 30–45 minutes, stirring every 10–15 minutes to prevent sticking and burning, until it becomes deeply caramelised.

Add the salt, sugar and shrimp paste, if using. Stir well and continue cooking for about 5 minutes. Once the colour is a deep, rich red, remove the sambal from the heat and allow to cool in the pan for 1 hour. This will keep in a sterilised glass jar (see page 25) or an airtight container in the fridge for up to 2 weeks.

THE TREE
OF LIFE

A COCONUT GROVE IN DAWAN

I've been brought to Dawan in east Bali by an ethnobotanist friend, Made, who works for a traditional textile organisation back in Ubud. We arrive at a seemingly empty coconut plantation. A hen and her chicks scuttle behind some shrubbery as we approach the only structure on the property — a rickety bamboo hut with a tattered electoral banner draped across the entrance. We peer behind the smiling candidate and see a mud stove flickering unattended. Made sources coconut sugar from this particular grove to use as a natural setting agent at the end of the indigo dying process. He fixes his gaze at the fronds above us. 'He must be climbing,' he says.

Eventually, we hear a scraping sound to our left. It's the man we've come to see, local priest and sugar maker Pak Mangku Sugata, sliding down a nearby palm. 'Good morning,' he says, adjusting the sickle tucked into the back of his shorts, 'are you here for tuak?'

Tuak is a type of palm wine made from the sap of the coconut tree. To make it, a hole is pierced into the upper core of the palm near the blossoms, from which pale golden nectar streams into a container overnight. The next day, the liquid is collected and stirred with kapur sirih (limestone paste) and a splinter of jackfruit tree bark, which ferments the beverage and gives it a milky, pink tinge. Pak Mangku Sugata pours us a pint. It's floral, frothy and bright on the palate.

Tuak is just one of the many gifts of the coconut palm. In fact, the plant is often dubbed the Tree of Life for its myriad cultural and culinary uses. Pak Mangku Sugata invites us into the soot-licked kitchen behind the curtain where he makes Gula Bali (page 98) – a rich, dark coconut sugar that lends its sweetness to many of the island's desserts and refreshments. He places an aluminium wok over the fire. 'It's better if you use a clay pan,' he says, 'but it takes too long.' This batch needs to cook for another four hours.

We sit by the burning hearth, watching the morning's nectar yield bubble and reduce. Pak Mangku Sugata throws half-a-dozen sela (sweet potatoes) into the syrupy mix, which is boiling away slowly, taking on its sweetness. While he mans the pan we visit a home down the road, where a family is producing everything from Santen (coconut milk, page 94) and Lengis (coconut oil, page 97) to telengis – a rich by-product of the oil-making process that is mixed with spices, grilled in little banana-leaf parcels and sold at the markets as a snack. Behind the house, leftover coconut shells are shaped into bowls, containers and cooking ladles. The husks are used to power the stoves.

Almost no part of the coconut plant goes unused in Bali. The straight, hardy trunk is a popular building material and the young and older fronds (known as busung and slepan, respectively) are woven into offerings and striking decorative pieces for ceremonies, parties and special events. Kuwud (young coconuts) are prized for their deeply hydrating, stomach-soothing liquid inside their pale green shells. Their opaque, jelly-like flesh is eaten fresh or scraped into drinks and iced desserts. Nyuh (mature coconuts), however, are the real stars of Balinese cooking. The rich white meat is roasted, grated and tossed through urab (see page 132) or lawar (see page 240) and massaged into ceremonial sate mixtures. Many Balinese soups gain their richness from hand-squeezed coconut milk.

In rituals, the coconut represents completeness and cleansing, among many other things. The juices of the just-developed fruits, known as bungkak, are sprinkled over the heads of devotees in an act of purification before ritual prayer. After we're born, the placenta is placed in the shell of a mature coconut and buried in the soil. And when we die, our ashes are held in a yellow coconut and released into the sea. So, the humble coconut carries us from the cradle to the grave, so to speak, keeping us sheltered, blessed and well-nourished in between.

Back at the sugar refinery, Pak Mangku Sugata is removing cooled half-spheres of gula Bali from their moulds (which are, of course, made from coconut shells). He sends us off with two bags of sugar cakes and a litre of tuak for good measure. 'To keep you well,' he says.

COCONUT GUIDE

When you're cooking Balinese food on a regular basis, it's almost guaranteed that you'll be opening a lot of coconuts. Even if you're not planning on making your own Santen (coconut milk, page 94) or Coconut oil (page 97), many recipes contain grated coconut meat from mature coconuts, so there's really no avoiding the task. On that note, we strongly recommend that you do make your own coconut milk. It's cleaner in flavour, has a more natural consistency and is obviously fresher than store-bought. It's also free of thickeners, added sugars and preservatives, which have no place in the paon.

MATURE
COCONUTS

A good coconut will have bright white flesh and a neutral, subtly sweet aroma. When you're working with mature coconuts, be sure to have a surplus on hand in case one is spoiled – particularly if they're imported and you can't tell how fresh they are. You'll know a coconut is spoiled if it smells fermented or if there's a purplish, pinkish or brown quality to the meat.

OPENING
METHODS

Opening a coconut the traditional way can be intimidating, so we've offered two methods.

Hand-held method: Hold the coconut in your non-dominant hand over a large mixing bowl to collect the water, and a heavy knife or cleaver blade in the other. You want to be hitting against the grain of the shell, so make sure you lay the coconut sideways in your hand, with the eyes facing outwards.

Using the back (or blunt) edge of the knife, hit the shell in the middle, against the grain, turning the coconut around after each heavy blow, until the shell cracks open. It may take a few goes before the shell finally splits. The aim is for it to break into two even-ish halves. We don't often use the water for cooking, however, it's nice to drink it instead of throwing it away.

Once the shell has split, you can repeat the same process with the halves to break them into quarters, which makes it easier to separate the meat from the shell. Prise the meat away from the shell using the sharp top corner of a cleaver blade, gently wiggling between the flesh and the shell until they break away from each other (see image next page).

Tea towel method: Start by draining the coconut water. Use the sharp end of a hammer to drill holes into the eyes at the top of the coconut. Pour the water into a glass or bowl and set aside.

Make a stand for the coconut by spinning or rolling up a tea towel and forming a ring on a solid counter surface or on the ground. Place the coconut on top of the towel ring – it should stay in place nicely here – on its side with the eyes facing to the side to ensure you will be whacking it against the grain of the shell.

Use a hammer to crack the shell open, swivelling the coconut around as you go until the shell gives way.

YOUNG COCONUTS

A couple of the drinks and desserts in this book call for young coconuts, which are normally pale green or yellow-green with fleshier outsides and jelly-like meat on the inside. In Bali, we often drink the water and scoop the flesh out as a snack. The best way to open a young coconut is to create a wide-mouthed lid of sorts on top, so that the meat can be easily accessed with a tablespoon. To do this safely, place the coconut on a solid surface (preferably the ground), hold it still with one hand and use the other to hack out the lid using a sharp, heavy knife or cleaver. Apply strong, deep, diagonal blows which go down and inwards as opposed to straight across the top, swivelling the coconut around with each blow. Some young coconuts have quite thick, fleshy shells, so keep going until you feel it start to give way. Once you're able to remove the top, pour the water into a jug and scoop the flesh out into a mixing bowl.

A gentler option is to use the tea towel method (see previous page). Just make a ring wide enough to support the coconut and hack, or carve, the top off using a sharp knife or cleaver.

Once you've separated the water and flesh, you can combine them with ice to make Es kuwud (page 231) or keep and consume them separately.

ROASTED COCONUT

Open the coconut (see previous page), break the shell into quarters and prise the meat out of the shell using the sharp corner of a cleaver.

Roast the coconut meat over an open flame or a gas burner for about 4 minutes on each side, or until it's nice and golden. It will smell sweet and slightly charred when ready. Don't worry about any burnt bits, you can easily scrape them off with a knife. Set the coconut aside to cool.

Grate the coconut using a box grater or a traditional pangikihan (page 38). Finely grate for things like urabs (see page 132) and coarsely grate for things like lawar (see page 240).

Makes 300 ml (10 fl oz)

— muslin (cheesecloth;
   optional)

— 1 small coconut (about
   450–500 g / 14 oz–1 lb 2 oz)
— 300 ml (10 fl oz) water

This is a simple, low-tech recipe for homemade santen (coconut milk), which is used in many Balinese dishes – from soups and stews to traditional cakes and sweet beverages. It comes through in a more subtle way than it does in, say, Thai cooking, but it plays a leading role nonetheless. To amp up the flavour and add smokiness, roast the coconut meat over charcoals or the flame of a gas stove before you grate it.

SANTEN
COCONUT MILK

Crack the coconut open using the back of a heavy cleaver (see page 91). Break the halves into quarters and prise the shell away using the sharpest edge of the cleaver.

If roasting the coconut, use the guide on page 92.

Finely grate the coconut meat into a small mixing bowl using a traditional pangikihan (page 38), the small holes of a box grater or a microplane. You want it to be as powdery as possible, almost like desiccated coconut, but fresh.

Add the water to the grated coconut. Hold the bowl down with one hand and use the other to combine the two ingredients, squeezing the juices of the coconut into the water for about 1–5 minutes, depending on how rich you like your coconut milk.

Strain the mixture through a cheesecloth or a fine-mesh sieve.

Santen is best used straight away, but you can store it in the fridge for up to 2 days.

Note

We'll forgive you for using a blender to save time. You'll need a high-speed blender, as a low-speed (3 speed) blender will not be powerful enough. If you absolutely must use store-bought coconut milk, shop around and buy the highest quality coconut milk you can find, preferably one with no thickeners and stabilisers. We prefer the brands Ayam and Chaokoh.

Makes 1 litre (34 fl oz/4 cups)

— 2 muslins (cheesecloths),
  about 30 × 30 cm/12 × 12 in

— meat of 6 mature coconuts,
  finely grated
— 6 litres (203 fl oz/24 cups)
  water
— ½ cm (¼ in) piece fresh
  turmeric, crushed (see
  page 28; optional)

'The best Balinese food is always cooked with homemade lengis nyuh (coconut oil). According to my mother and aunt, there are two classic methods for making coconut oil. The first method is to simply simmer coconut milk over a wood fire for 3–4 hours. The second method uses the sun as the heat source to separate the oil from the milk. Using mature coconuts (see page 91) is key, as they deliver the most flavour – these are dark in colour with dry husks. Another secret from my family kitchen is to leave the copra (the thin layer of brown skin between the shell and the meat) on the coconut meat as it contains the best fats. We sometimes add turmeric for colour and flavour, and to help the oil keep on the shelf for longer, but it's not essential. Here is a slightly modified version of my grandmother's lengis nyuh recipe.'

— *Wayan*

LENGIS NYUH
COCONUT OIL

In a large tub or mixing bowl, combine the coconut with 4 litres (135 fl oz/16 cups) of the water and let it soak for 10 minutes.

Using both hands, squeeze the water and coconut together continuously for 15–20 minutes, until the liquid becomes rich, opaque and milky.

Pour the coconut milk through a wire sieve lined with cheesecloth into another large tub or mixing bowl, pressing the pulp with your hand until all the liquid has been strained and the pulp feels dry. Set the liquid aside and transfer the pulp back to the tub or bowl used for soaking.

Combine the strained pulp with the remaining 2 litres (68 fl oz/ 8 cups) water, let it soak for 10–15 minutes and repeat the steps above. Discard the pulp.

Pour the strained coconut milk into a large stockpot and add the turmeric, if using. Bring the liquid to the boil over a high heat, then reduce the heat to low and simmer for 2–3 hours, stirring every 15 minutes or so to keep the milk from overflowing. It is ready when the oil and the milk have visibly separated and the transparent, yellowish oil has risen to the surface.

Leave the liquid to cool in the pot for at least 1 hour.

Use a ladle to carefully skim all the oil from the surface, and transfer it into a jar or container. Store the oil in a glass jar at room temperature (it will harden in the fridge) for up to 1 week.

Makes 350 ml (12 fl oz)

— 300 g (10½ oz) palm sugar,
  coarsely chopped
— 100 ml (3½ fl oz) water
— 2 pandan leaves

This thick, stringy coconut palm sugar syrup is good enough to eat straight up with a spoon. We pour it over everything from jaja (traditional cakes and sweets) and deep-fried bananas to roasted cassava, taro and yams. It's even great in tea or coffee. Different palms produce different flavoured sugars. Coconut palm sugar has a clean, almost savoury profile and is a darker brown than, say, lontar and aren palm sugars (for more information, see page 276). For this recipe, we recommend finding a good-quality Indonesian coconut palm sugar.

GULA BALI

PALM SUGAR SYRUP

Place all the ingredients in a small saucepan and simmer over a medium heat for 10 minutes, or until it becomes a thin caramel-like sauce.

Strain the syrup into a sterilised glass bottle (see page 25) or bowl and set aside to cool. Dip and drizzle away. The syrup keeps for 1 week at room temperature, or for up to 2 months in the fridge.

Makes 1 kg (2 lb 3 oz)

— 500 ml (17 fl oz/2 cups)
  vegetable oil
— 1 kg (2 lb 3 oz/4 cups)
  shelled, raw peanuts
— ½ tablespoon sea salt

You can use fried peanuts as a side, a snack or to make peanut sauce. They're sold in little packets at most warungs (local eateries) and are paired with a type of sweet roasted coconut condiment called Saur kuning (page 247) on special occasions.

KACANG TANAH GORENG
FRIED PEANUTS

Heat the oil in a wok over a medium heat for about 5 minutes. Slowly add the peanuts and fry, stirring constantly so that all the peanuts cook evenly, for about 8–12 minutes, or until golden-brown.

Remove the peanuts using a spider ladle or slotted spoon and place on a tray lined with paper towel to drain off excess oil.

Sprinkle the peanuts with the salt and store in a glass container for 3–4 days.

Makes 250 g (9 oz)

— 500 g (1 lb 2 oz) small, dry
  red beans (any kind) or chilli
  beans
— 500 ml (17 fl oz/2 cups)
  vegetable oil
— 1 teaspoon sea salt

This condiment is often served with Saur kuning (page 247). Sprouted beans are smaller and earthier than kacang tanah (peanuts) and have a considerable amount of crunch. You'll need to soak and sprout the beans first, so start this recipe a day or two ahead.

KACANG MENTIK GORENG
FRIED SPROUTED BEANS

Place the beans in a tub or large bowl along with 1 litre (34 fl oz/ 4 cups) water to rehydrate for about 10 hours.

Strain the beans and line the empty tub with thick, damp paper towel. Place the beans on top and cover with more damp paper towel. Let the beans sit at room temperature overnight, at least 12 hours. The beans are ready when they have sprouted and have a fresh, crunchy texture.

Heat the oil in a wok over a medium heat for about 8 minutes, or until it reaches smoke point, then slowly add the sprouted beans. Fry the beans for about 8–12 minutes, stirring constantly, until they're crisp and golden-brown.

Remove the beans from the oil with a spider ladle or slotted spoon and place on a tray lined with a paper towel to soak up excess oil. Sprinkle with the salt and store in an airtight jar for up to 2 weeks.

NAWA SANGA

THE NINE EXPRESSIONS OF THE SUPREME GOD

In Balinese Hinduism, the Nawa Sanga is often referred to as a spiritual compass of sorts. It is a depiction of the nine expressions or manifestations of god, which come together to represent the greater universe, or macrocosmos, and acts as a guidepost for humankind so that we might be able to understand how to keep the cosmic balance in order. The Nawa Sanga reminds us that there is diversity in completeness, that the universe is a multi-layered amalgamation of the various traits and characteristics of the supreme, each with its own function in the inner workings of our lives.

There are nine gods in a state of perfect balance – Iswara, Mahesora, Brahma, Rudra, Mahadewa, Sangkara, Wisnu, Sambu and Siwa – each with its own direction, colour, sacred weapon, number, part of the body, even day of the week. Each of the nine gods represents different expressions of the supreme god, Ida Sanghyang Widhi Wasa: the ultimate power of the universe whom our prayers are directed to at the end of the day. Every manifestation plays a unique role in both the macrocosmos and the microcosmos, and allows the work of Ida Sanghyang Widhi Wasa to become recognisable around us and within us – from the way our organs function in the body to the way the natural elements work to how we should adorn offerings for specific ritual purposes.

The colouring of lawar (see page 240) is a wonderful food-based example of this. In other offerings, naturally coloured or dyed rice is used to nod to these divine expressions. Of the nine manifestations, there are three that are the most revered: Brahma, Wisnu and Siwa – The Creator, The Preserver and The Destroyer, respectively. They are known collectively as the Trimurti (triple deity), and their colours – red, black and white – are interwoven throughout our cultural lives. The holy trinity of Brahma, Wisnu and Siwa is so significant because it represents the cycle of all things. So, by acknowledging them, we are able to digest the rhythms of all things, including that of the paon – where Brahma rules the fire and Wisnu the water.

FROM
THE FIELDS

–

FROM
THE FIELDS

–

FROM
THE FIELDS

–

FROM
THE FIELDS

–

FROM
THE FIELDS

–

FROM
THE FIELDS

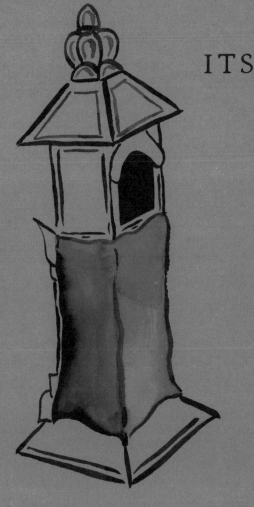

RICE IN

ITS VARIOUS

FORMS

RICE

THE SEEDS OF CONSCIOUSNESS

I remember sitting on my father's lap as
a child at the temple, showered in holy
water, having just completed our prayers.
He took a generous pinch of soaked
uncooked rice, known ceremonially as bija,
and pressed it between my brows, on each
temple and just above my collarbone.
Then he picked out a few whole grains and
placed them in the palm of my right hand.
'Put these in your mouth,' he said. 'Swallow
them, but don't chew.' I, however, rarely
listened to the final instruction.

For many years, I carried out this practice without truly understanding the meaning behind it. When I was a bit older, I finally asked the question, 'What is bija for?' 'Bija,' my father said, 'is Sanskrit for seed.' In Bali we believe grains of rice are descended from the heavens and that the consciousness of Siwa sprouts from these seeds – the god of destruction, reproduction and renewal. 'From your third eye, the bija will bring you wisdom,' he said, 'at your temples they represent balance, at your throat, they will provide energy, and the seeds that you swallow represent completeness, which is why they shouldn't be broken by your teeth.' From that moment onwards I stopped chewing my bija.

To understand the symbolism behind the humble rice grain – how it originated from the skies, bringing with it not only food but culture, prosperity and even its own unique deity, the rice goddess Dewi Sri – is to understand its significance to Bali. Once upon a time, a good part of the island's lowlands were etched with vast fields and towering terraces of slow-growing strains of heirloom rice and the dry-growing rice known as padi gogo. The colours of the landscape were tuned to the maturity of the crops, transitioning from brown to electric green and eventually bright yellow at harvest. Daily life, too, moved to the rhythm of the rice-growing cycle, which in turn dictated the cultural calendar alongside the seasons, the planets and the stars.

Although heritage rice farming is less prominent in Bali today (thanks to colonisation, tourism and the Green Revolution of the '70s, which introduced fertilisers, pesticides and fast-growing, high-yielding crops), the plant remains deeply revered and its popularity on our dining plates, one could safely say, has only increased with its wider availability. We consume mountains of the stuff – in cakes, with soups, topped with fried eggs, slow-cooked into congee-like porridges, or simply dressed with warm coconut oil, sea salt and Sambal matah (page 76).

Rice also remains an irreplaceable spiritual tool. Sometimes it's dished out on small squares of banana leaf to feed the elemental or lower energies of the family compound – the spirits – in daily offerings known as saiban. Other times, several colours and varieties of the grain (red, black, white and yellow) are shaped into wong-wongan, small human forms made to ward off negativity, sickness and evil. The crops themselves are routinely blessed in carefully timed rituals directed towards the rice goddess, Dewi Sri. There are many tales of her emergence. One simple version of the story is that the first rice sprouted when Sinta and Rama – incarnations of the Earth Mother Pertiwi and The Preserver, Wisnu – came together as ashes and water, respectively. The seed-bearing grass that rose from their communion was considered divine and is personified by this radiant earth deity. From then onwards, rice and its cultivation became a link to the heavens with Dewi Sri as its revered protector. She now appears in carvings, paintings and statues across the island. Numerous hotels, restaurants and even a brand of local palm and rice wines carry her name. Once, when I found myself in an accident on a road skirted by rice fields, a farmer from the area told me to go home and ask Dewi Sri for forgiveness for having caused calamity in the realm of her newly sprouting crops. So, her influence touches all Balinese worshippers, regardless of their direct connection to the agricultural world. She is fertility, bounty and prosperity, in the same way that rice is a bridge to the earth, wealth and, most importantly, nourishment.

Makes 2 kg (4 lb 6 oz)

- 1 kg (2 lb 3 oz) white or
  red rice
- 1 tablespoon sea salt
  (optional)

Steamed rice is fairly simple in theory – all you need is grains, heat, water and a bit of patience. You can boil it – you can even throw it in a rice-cooker – but in Bali we are rice connoisseurs and neither of these methods will suffice. The best cooks prepare rice the traditional way using a dangdang (see page 37) over a wood fire, which makes for smoky, fluffy grains that are soft on the outside and firm enough on the inside to provide a good amount of bite. This recipe uses the traditional method of cooking rice, where the grains are cooked twice and given time in-between to rest and steep, to slowly absorb as much moisture as possible.

It's important to note that rice isn't naturally shiny white. In its unprocessed state it has valuable husks (red, white or black) that contain most of the plant's nutritional properties. Processed white rice, however, has become fashionable in Indonesia – perceived as a more sophisticated food. It is delicious, but natural rice is far more textural, flavourful and more nutritious. Many health-conscious cooks will choose beras merah (unhulled grains) over processed rice any day. We strongly encourage you to experiment with both. Please note that this method does not work well with smaller quantities of rice, but the rice can be stored in a rice cooker on the warming setting or in a bamboo basket to serve throughout the day, or store it in the fridge for up to 2 days to make fried rice.

NASI PUTIH OR NASI MERAH

TRADITIONAL STEAMED WHITE OR RED RICE

Rinse the rice under running tap water in a large strainer until the water runs almost clear. Transfer the rice to a large mixing bowl, cover with water and leave to soak for 15 minutes.

Meanwhile, fill a medium or large steamer pot with water to about 2½ cm (1 in) below the steamer basket. Bring to the boil.

Strain the rice and transfer it to the steamer pot. Cover and steam for 15 minutes for white rice or 25 minutes for red rice.

Return the rice to the mixing bowl, then quickly pour hot water from the pot over the rice until it's just submerged. Cover the bowl and allow the rice to soak to absorb the water for about 15–20 minutes. We call this process aru.

Add enough fresh water to the steamer pot to sit 2½ cm (1 in) below the steamer basket and bring to the boil.

Give the rice a stir to loosen the grains and add the salt, then transfer it back into the steamer pot, cover and steam for a further 20 minutes, or 30 minutes if you're cooking red or brown rice. When the rice is done, it should be fluffy, but not sticky, and easy to serve.

Makes 2 kg (4 lb 6 oz)

- 1 kg (2 lb 3 oz) white rice
- 100 ml (3½ fl oz) Air kunyit
  (page 70)
- 150 ml (5 fl oz) Santen
  (coconut milk, page 94)
- 4 garlic cloves, crushed
  (see page 28)
- 2 lemongrass stems, crushed
  and knotted (see page 28)
- 1 cm (½ in) piece of fresh
  galangal, thickly sliced and
  crushed (see page 28)
- 2 teaspoons sea salt

Colour plays an important role in our cultural and culinary lives. In the Nawa Sanga, Bali's sacred directional compass (for more information, see page 102), kuning (yellow) represents Mahadewa (the god of the west), so, in some ceremonial contexts, turmeric rice is used to honour this energy. From a non-religious standpoint, it's a celebratory dish, making appearances at birthdays, anniversaries and family gatherings alike. On top of all this, it's very good for you – every mouthful is brimming with healthy fats from the coconut oil and anti-inflammatory and cooling properties from the turmeric. It's a bright, medicinal, deeply meaningful special occasion star. Please note that this method does not work well with smaller quantities of rice, but the rice can be stored in a rice cooker on the warming setting or in a bamboo basket to serve throughout the day, or store it in the fridge for up to 2 days.

NASI KUNING
YELLOW RICE

Rinse the rice under running tap water in a large strainer until the water runs almost clear. Transfer the rice to a large mixing bowl, cover it with water and leave to soak for 15 minutes.

Meanwhile, fill a medium or large steamer pot with water to about 2½ cm (1 in) below the steamer basket. Bring to the boil.

Strain the rice and transfer it to the steamer pot. Cover and steam the rice for 15 minutes.

Meanwhile, add 800 ml (27 fl oz) water, the turmeric water and the coconut milk to a large saucepan and bring to the boil.

Return the rice to the mixing bowl and pour over the hot turmeric–coconut milk. Add the remaining ingredients and stir everything together slowly until all of the ingredients are evenly combined. Cover the bowl and let the rice steep for 20 minutes, or until all of the liquid has been absorbed.

Bring the water in the steamer pot to the boil again, and stir the rice with a wooden spoon to loosen the grains. Transfer the rice back to the steamer, cover and steam for an additional 20 minutes, or until the rice is fully cooked. When ready, the nasi kuning will be fluffy, fragrant and brilliant yellow in colour.

Makes 1.5 kg (3 lb 5 oz)

— 600 g (1 lb 5 oz) white rice
— 2 sweet potatoes, cut into
½ cm (¼ in) cubes

Nasi sela is a nostalgic dish for many Balinese. It used to be common in the regencies of Gianyar, Tabanan and Badung – a staple food that kept the masses nourished through times of economic hardship and natural disasters. As rice became easier to access, the art of combining it with little chunks of sela (sweet potato) became less popular. It was labelled as a dish for the struggling – a peasant food – but it's since had somewhat of a comeback and is being reproduced by warungs (local eateries) and home cooks alike. The sela provides a gentle sweetness that pairs well with seafood and grilled meats, but it's also dense and hearty enough to serve with vegetables alone. The key to a good nasi sela is making sure neither the rice nor the sweet potato is overcooked – you want both ingredients to retain their individual shapes and textures. Serve it in place of plain rice to make a meal more interesting.

NASI SELA
SWEET POTATO RICE

Rinse the rice under running tap water in a large strainer until the water runs almost clear. Transfer the rice to a large mixing bowl, cover with water and leave to soak for 15 minutes.

Meanwhile, fill a medium or large steamer pot with water to about 2½ cm (1 in) below the steamer basket. Bring to the boil.

Strain the rice and transfer it to the steamer pot. Cover and steam the rice for 15 minutes.

Return the rice to the mixing bowl. Rinse the sweet potato to remove some of the starches and add it to the rice in the bowl. Give it a stir and pour the hot water from the steamer pot over the rice and sweet potato until they are just submerged. Stir again, cover the bowl and let it steep for about 20 minutes.

Add enough fresh water to the steamer pot to sit 2½ cm (1 in) below the steamer basket and bring to the boil. Stir the rice and sweet potato mix with a wooden spoon to loosen the grains and return the mixture to the steamer. Cover and steam for another 20 minutes.

Makes 1.2 kg (2 lb 10 oz)

- 250 g (9 oz) white rice
- 250 g (9 oz) ground yellow or white corn

Starch, namely rice, is the heart of any Balinese meal. In drier parts of Bali, such as Nusa Penida, where both rain and rice are scarce, corn and cassava are the key carbohydrates. Corn is harvested, dried and stored in the wetter months to be enjoyed during the dry months. Nasi jagung is a mix of corn and white rice that pairs nicely with soupy dishes such as Kuah pindang (page 193). The ground corn kernels not only make the rice more substantial but also provide a different texture, little bursts of sweetness and a nice pop of colour.

NASI JAGUNG
CORN RICE

Rinse the rice and corn under running tap water in a large strainer until the water runs almost clear. Transfer to a large mixing bowl, cover with water and leave to soak for 10 minutes.

Meanwhile, fill a medium or large steamer pot with water to about 2½ cm (1 in) below the steamer basket. Bring to the boil.

Strain the rice and corn, transfer to the steamer pot and use your finger to make a small hole in the middle to allow the steam to circulate through the rice and bounce off the lid to cook the rice evenly. Cover the pot with a lid and steam for about 15 minutes.

Return the rice and corn mix to the mixing bowl, then quickly pour hot water from the pot over the rice until it is just submerged. Cover the bowl and allow the rice to soak for 15 minutes to absorb the water. We call this process aru.

Add enough fresh water to the steamer pot to sit 2½ cm (1 in) below the steamer basket and bring to the boil.

Give the mix a stir to loosen the grains, then transfer it back to the steamer and make a hole in the middle with your finger. Cover the pot and steam it for an additional 20 minutes. When it is done, the rice will be fluffy in texture with yellow speckles from the corn. Keep it warm in a rice cooker or store it in a covered bamboo basket to serve throughout the day.

In the paon, rice is rarely kept for more than a day. Old rice is considered inedible and normally ends up as animal food. Now that most people have refrigeration, sometimes the odd bowl of rice does make it to the following day. When that is the case, it might be fried into nasi goreng, or it might be flavoured with red (Asian) shallots, garlic and chillies, maybe even chicken or fish, then wrapped in leaves and grilled into these soft, hearty nasi bakar rice parcels. We've recommended white rice for this recipe, but you could also use red or brown rice.

Place two salam leaves along the grain in each parcel.

Add a large handful of the rice mixture on top, leaving 2½ cm (1 in) free around the filling.

Top each pile of rice with a big spoonful of the sambal.

Fold the banana leaves over the filling. Work with the veins of the leaves, not against them, so they don't tear.

Roll the leaves into a log.

Fasten one end with a toothpick. Stand the parcel upright with the fastened end down, and give it a soft tap on the table to pack down the ingredients. Fasten the other end.

- 4 banana leaves
  (20 × 20 cm/8 × 8 in)
- toothpicks

- 280 g (10 oz) cooked white
  rice (for a recipe, see
  page 111)
- 1 tablespoon coconut oil
  (for a recipe, see page 97)
- 2 red (Asian) shallots, finely
  chopped
- 6 garlic cloves, finely
  chopped
- 4 tabasco chillies, finely
  chopped
- 2 teaspoons sea salt
- pinch of ground white
  pepper
- 4 salam leaves
- 100 g (3½ oz/½ cup)
  Pindang sambal tomat
  (page 200), roughly shredded

NASI BAKAR
GRILLED RICE

Place the rice in a mixing bowl and set it aside to come to room temperature.

Heat the oil in a wok over a medium heat and sauté the shallots, garlic and chilli until fragrant. Remove from the wok with a spider ladle or slotted spoon and combine with the rice. Add the salt and pepper and mix everything together. Set aside.

Prepare the banana leaves for wrapping (see page 27) and use the guide opposite to wrap the filling in the leaves.

Preheat a barbecue or grill (broiler) and place the parcels sambal-side up. Over a medium heat, grill for 8 minutes. Turn over the parcels and cook for another 8 minutes, or until the rice inside is hot, steaming and fragrant. Be careful not to burn the leaves.

Place each parcel, sambal-side up, on a serving plate and carefully open them. Eat them while they're hot.

Tip

Ayam sisit (page 152) also works nicely in this recipe. To make the dish meat-free you can swap the pindang for Tempe manis (page 164).

- 4 banana leaves (20 × 20 cm/ 8 × 8 in) (see Tip)
- toothpicks, bamboo sticks or butcher's twine

- 400 g (14 oz/2½ cups) steamed white rice (for a recipe, see page 111)
- Tipat cantok (page 219), to serve
- Serosop (page 201), to serve
- sate, to serve (see page 220)

There are generally two kinds of savoury rice cakes in Bali. The first is known as tipat and is made from uncooked rice steamed inside diamond-shaped pouches woven out of young palm leaves. The second is known as lontong and is made from cooked rice wrapped in banana leaves in the shape of a log. Both are boiled to form dense, sticky, savoury rice cakes that pair wonderfully with sates and other soupy or saucy dishes.

Tipat double as offering foods and often appear on ceremonial or celebratory menus. The coconut-leaf parcels that they're traditionally cooked and served in are deftly woven and can only be mastered by practice. To attempt them from step-by-step instructions alone would likely result in a strong headache, a burst of anger and maybe even tears (and, as we know from the wisdom of the paon, this is not a desirable outcome), so, we'll just share the instructions for lontong, which are equally delicious and pair well with a number of recipes in this book.

LONTONG
BOILED RICE CAKES

Prepare the banana leaves for wrapping (see page 27) and use the guide opposite to wrap the filling in the banana leaves.

Place the parcels in a medium stockpot along with 3 litres (101 fl oz/ 12 cups) water and bring to the boil. Cook the parcels over a medium heat for about 2 hours, or until the logs are firm but the rice inside the leaves still gives way when you give it a gentle squeeze.

Remove the lontongs from the pot using tongs and place on a rack to cool completely. Carefully unwrap the parcels, slice the rice cakes and serve them with tipat cantok, serosop and sate.

Tip

Buy more banana leaves than you'll need in case some tear while wrapping the parcels. Unused banana leaves can be stored in the freezer.

Place a quarter of the steamed rice in each parcel along the grain of the banana leaves.

Fold the leaves over the filling and roll into a log. Work with the veins of the leaves, not against them, so they don't tear.

You can fasten the ends with a toothpick (or a thin bamboo stick if you want to use the traditional way), or tie them shut with butcher's twine, nice and tight — you want to make sure water won't enter the parcel when cooking. Ensure there are no tears in the banana leaves.

FROM THE
LAND

–

FROM THE
LAND

–

FROM THE
LAND

–

FROM THE
LAND

–

FROM THE
LAND

–

FROM THE
LAND

DISHES

FROM THE

MOUNTAINS

AND

LOWLANDS

EDIBLE EDENS

THE SACRED MOUNTAIN, FOOD FORESTS AND NATIVE PLANTS

Somebody once told me a story that inspired me to climb a mountain. They said that at some point during the eighth century, an Indian sage by the name of Rsi Markandeya came to Bali by way of Java, and Hinduism touched the island's shores for the very first time. His initial take on the landscape was that it was long and thin, until he climbed Bali's tallest peak, Mount Agung, and saw the island for what it really was – wide and undulating from east to west, narrowing and expanding again slightly towards the south. A mass of smaller mountains rose from the middle of the land like the spine of a dragon. Any signs of human life were probably concealed beneath the vast stretches of jungle. I'm yet to confirm the accuracy of this tale, but it makes for a beautiful story nonetheless.

Mount Agung is both a wonderful vantage point and a highly sacred landmark. Most Balinese Hindus revere it as the throne of the gods. Besakih, Bali's largest temple, sits majestically at its base, a sprawling devotional city of sorts, frequented by people from all stretches of the land on important ritual dates and pilgrimages. Many Hindu compounds have shrines facing the direction of the great mountain. It is the ultimate symbol of creation — a sky-scraping altar of Mother Nature's own design. It's also an active volcano that has spewed hot ash, rocks and lava across and beyond the isle, burying villages, destroying crops and remoulding the shape of the land time and time again over the years. However, some years after the deluge, blessed mineral-rich earth emerges, which turns the island's valleys hyper-fertile and teeming with edible treasures. So, it's no wonder, then, that Agung is worshipped to the point that rice, sweets and even meats are sometimes wrapped, pinched and moulded into peak-shaped delicacies in its honour. This mountain is in many ways the vital source of Bali's lushness and bounty.

From its summit, over 3000 metres (9840 feet) into the sky, rice-fields roll out over the agricultural lowlands like green-and-gold patchwork quilts. Rivers twist and flow like sparkling veins towards the coastline, and food forests, known as tegals, burst from the undeveloped parts of residential villages. These pockets of green remain a prominent part of traditional village life and are the source of many of Bali's most intriguing foods. The likes of jackfruit, durian, several varieties of banana, young fiddlehead ferns, star fruit trees, wani (white mangoes), cloves, taro and more sprout abundantly and freely within these edible Edens. Southern Bali, by comparison, is a clutter of red and brown tiled roofs and vast resort lands that twinkle like tangled fairy lights by nightfall — the scars of mass tourism, hardcore development and bottomless beer consumption.

In the tegals, cows help fertilise the soil, lean chickens roam freely, controlling pests, laying eggs and sometimes ending up on the dinner table (or in a pile of offerings, should they be of the suitable colour and heirloom breed). Tegals tie into many parts of daily life in Bali, from providing us with a free-for-all pantry of fruit, vegetables and spices, to crafting materials such as bamboo, the young shoots of which are used for cooking, and older rafts are excellent poles for ceremonial offerings and building structures.

Adults and children alike come to these forests to forage and be with nature, returning to the kitchen with everything from wild greens for urabs (see page 132) or lawar (see page 240) to fruits for rujak (see page 165) and palm nectar to distil into arak (traditional palm wine). Every ingredient is harvested based on nature's willingness to provide it — without force, chemicals or too much human interference. And so, each visit to the forest is laden with surprises, and the meal that comes from it symbolises the generosity of the natural world.

Most of the plants that grow within these tegals are unique to Bali and some other parts of the archipelago. We haven't been able to include all of them in our recipes, but it's important to talk about them as they are the real stars of the paon. Many of these ingredients were once common foods, such as mango leaves, star fruit leaves and banana trunk (see following pages), which my parents and my niang recall eating often in the days before supermarkets. And quite a few of them, as you'll discover, also double as potent medicines from the earth.

RARE EDIBLE PLANTS

These are the heirloom ingredients of the paon – the kind of things our grandparents' generation would have foraged and cooked on a regular basis, before the convenience of supermarkets, local grocers and big agriculture. Many cooks still work with them, but nowhere as often as they used to. These days, you'll mainly find them in rural home kitchens, some specialist warungs (local eateries) or as part of a spread for special occasions.

These plants grow wild – for the most part in the jungle, private gardens and tegals – and many are also used as natural medicinal remedies. Some are classified as cold foods, which means they have a general cooling effect on the body, soothing the liver, settling the stomach and lowering inflammation. Others are heating, which means they create warmth in the body, stimulating the digestion and getting the blood pumping.

BAMBOO SHOOTS, FRESH (EMBUNG)
Bamboo is rich in minerals such as silica, magnesium and sulphur. The fresh young shoots are often finely chopped or grated and made into urabs (see page 132), lawars (see page 240) and curries. Depending on what part of the island you're in, you might be served black, green or yellow bamboo prepared in any of the three ways above.

BANANA TREE TRUNK (ARES)
The trunk of banana trees can be finely sliced and incorporated into jukut (vegetable dishes).

BULUN BAON LEAVES (DON BULUN BAON)
An aromatic leaf that is used to brighten dishes such as Tepeng (page 130). It's got a very subtle perfume almost like a green tea.

CASSUMUNAR GINGER (BANGLE)
Part of the ginger family and related to galangal, this bright-yellow root is highly medicinal with anti-parasitic, anti-inflammatory and antibacterial properties.

CINNAMON LEAVES (DON KAYU MANIS)
These leaves are bright, sweet and grassy on the palate and are served as a vegetable or squeezed into a cooling Loloh kunyit (page 265).

COFFEE TREE LEAVES (DON KOPI)

Peppery leaves with a gentle sweetness and floral undertones.
Usually served as jukut (vegetable dishes) or boiled into a tea.

DALUMAN LEAVES (DON DALUMAN)

These cool, earthy leaves (*Cyclea barbata*) are hand-squeezed and left to
set into a soft, grassy jelly that's often served in coconut milk as a dessert
(see page 266).

MANGO LEAVES (DON POH)

Some types of mango leaves can be used as vegetables. They're grassy,
slightly bitter and work well in salads with spices and coconut.

MORINGA LEAVES (DON KELOR)

Used in soups, broths and urabs (see page 132), these small, round leaves
are full of antioxidants and high in chlorophyll and minerals. They're
mild, grassy and sweet in flavour.

NGAI CAMPHOR LEAVES (SEMBUNG)

Also known as balsam leaves, these are used in a variety of the medicinal
drinks known as Loloh kunyit (page 265) to cool the body, heal
respiratory conditions such as coughing, and balance wind conditions
such as bloating and distension.

PAPAYA LEAVES (DON GEDANG)

The leaves of the papaya tree are treated as vegetables. Super bitter
papaya leaf juice is also consumed to protect the liver and gallbladder
and to cool the blood, and is a popular remedy for dengue fever.

STAR FRUIT LEAVES (DON BELIMBING)
The dark-green, slightly bitter leaves are used in vegetable dishes such as lawar (see page 240). Star fruit is known to be a cooling plant that can help lower blood pressure.

SWEET RUSH (JANGU)
A rhizome that is used very sparingly in the aromatic spice combination Base wangen (page 54).

TURMERIC LEAVES (DON KUNYIT)
Turmeric leaves are used to wrap steamed meats in the north. They can also be used sparingly to bring perfume to seafood and chicken.

Serves 2

- 3 small garlic cloves,
  roughly chopped
- 1 candlenut, roasted and
  crushed (see pages 26 and 28)
- ½ cm (¼ in) piece fresh
  turmeric, roughly chopped
- thick slice of fresh lesser
  galangal, roughly chopped
- 1 tablespoon coconut oil
  (for a recipe, see page 97)
- 100 g (3½ oz) white rice
- 450 ml (15 fl oz) water or
  chicken stock (for a recipe,
  see page 73)
- sea salt, to taste
- hardboiled egg, to serve
- fresh chillies, to serve
- Sambal goreng (page 75),
  to serve (optional)

'Tepeng, or bubuh, as it's also known as, is our answer to congee – warm, homey and healing. My grandmother cooks tepeng every morning, throwing in a handful of rare and fragrant bulun baon leaves (see page 127) towards the end of the cooking process, which adds a lovely herbaceous flavour to the dish. Children, the elderly and anyone who's under the weather will be prescribed tepeng. In the morning markets, it's dressed up with fried peanuts, shredded chicken and generous helpings of sambal. Here is the simple spice-accented version we eat for breakfast at home.'

– Maya

TEPENG

SAVOURY RICE PORRIDGE

Crush the garlic, candlenut, turmeric and lesser galangal into a fine paste using a mortar and pestle. Stir the coconut oil into the paste and set aside.

Rinse the rice under running tap water in a large strainer until the water runs almost clear. Add the rice, water or stock and the spice paste to a medium saucepan and stir everything together. Bring the rice mixture to the boil and give it another stir to make sure the rice doesn't stick to the bottom of the pan. Reduce the heat to low and simmer for around 20–30 minutes, or until most of the water has evaporated and it resembles a thick porridge. Season to taste. The rice should be soft, yellow, savoury and gently spiced.

You can add a handful of leaves (such as bulun baon, salam leaves or daun kayu manis if you are able to source these, or alternatively you can use moringa leaves or spinach) at the very end of the cooking process and stir through until they're just wilted.

Serve warm with a hardboiled egg, chopped fresh chillies or sambal goreng.

Serves 6

- ½ tablespoon coconut oil
  (for a recipe, see page 97)
- 150 g (5½ oz/½ cup) Base
  genep (page 50)
- 500 g (1 lb 2 oz) chicken legs,
  skin on
- 1.5 litres (51 fl oz/6 cups)
  water
- 1 tablespoon sea salt
- 300 g (10½ oz) white rice
- 200 ml (7 fl oz) Santen
  (coconut milk, page 94)
- 7 salam leaves
- 1 lemongrass stem, crushed
  (see page 28)
- 240 g (8½ oz/1 cup) Urab
  kacang (page 134), to serve
- 60 g (2 oz/½ cup) Kacang
  tanah goreng (page 101)
  or Kacang mentik goreng
  (page 101), to serve
- Fried shallots (page 75),
  to serve

This rice porridge is a fancier version of bubuh (rice porridge) that hails from Buleleng in the island's north. It's cooked in coconut milk and dressed up with pulled chicken, chicken broth, lemongrass and salam leaves. It's super hearty, healing and full of interesting textures, flavours and aromas. We like to call it chicken porridge for the soul.

BUBUH MENGGUH
NORTHERN-STYLE RICE PORRIDGE

Heat the oil in a medium stockpot over a medium heat and sauté the base genep for 3–4 minutes.

Add the chicken and cook for a further 3–4 minutes. Add the water and salt and bring to the boil. Reduce the heat to low and simmer for about 1 hour, or until the chicken is fully cooked and fork-tender.

Remove the chicken from the pot using tongs and lay it on a rack to cool. Strain the stock through a fine-mesh sieve into a large bowl, discarding the sediment. Transfer 200 ml (7 fl oz) of the stock to another bowl and set aside for later, then return the remaining stock to the pot.

Rinse the rice under running tap water in a large strainer until the water runs almost clear.

Add the coconut milk to the pot and stir for 30 seconds to incorporate it fully. Add the rice, salam leaves and lemongrass and cook over a low heat, stirring occasionally to prevent any sticking or burning, and add small amounts of water if needed to smooth the texture, for about 45 minutes, or until it has turned into a porridge.

Remove the porridge from the heat and set aside.

Reheat the reserved stock and shred the chicken meat by hand and set aside.

To serve, evenly divide the porridge between six deep bowls and use the back of a spoon to press a shallow indent into the middle of the porridge. Then evenly divide the toppings between the bowls in the following order: first urab kacang, then the shredded chicken, then 1 tablespoon kacang goreng. Finish with about 1½ tablespoons of the stock poured over the top. Sprinkle with fried shallots and serve immediately.

Serves 4

- 220 g (8 oz / 1½ cups) finely
  grated roasted coconut
  (see page 92)
- 4 cucumbers, peeled, halved
  lengthways and sliced
- sea salt, to taste
- 4 lime leaves, finely sliced,
  to serve
- juice of ½ lime, to serve

SAMBAL
- 4 tablespoons coconut oil
  (for a recipe, see page 97)
- 4–5 red (Asian) shallots,
  finely sliced
- 5 garlic cloves, finely sliced
- 6 red bird's eye chillies,
  finely sliced (see page 274;
  optional)
- 1 teaspoon shrimp paste,
  rolled into a ball
- thumbnail-sized piece
  of lesser galangal, finely
  chopped
- 1 teaspoon salt

In Bali, we can make an urab out of just about anything – roots, shoots, fern tips, tree leaves, you name it. If it sings with coconut, it's a go. We've included a number of our favourite urab recipes here. This cucumber number normally comes out on special occasions. It's bright, refreshing and full of contrasting flavours. You can reduce or even leave out the chillies for less heat if you prefer.

URAB TIMUN
CUCUMBER AND BURNT COCONUT SALAD

To make the sambal, heat the oil in a small wok over a medium heat. Add the shallots and fry for 2 minutes, or until they become translucent. Add the garlic and fry, stirring constantly to make sure nothing sticks or burns, for 4 minutes, or until the garlic and shallots have gently caramelised.

Add the chilli, shrimp paste and lesser galangal and cook, stirring, until the shrimp paste is completely dissolved, the chilli is wilted and the lesser galangal becomes fragrant. Add the salt and stir again, then take off the heat.

Pour most of the sambal into a bowl, setting about a handful aside for seasoning, and combine it with the coconut using your fingers.

Add the cucumber and some of the coconut mixture to a large bowl and toss together using your hands. Massage it well but be careful not to bruise the cucumber too much, adding more coconut mixture until you're happy with the cucumber to coconut ratio. The cucumber should be nicely coated but not too soggy.

Season with salt to taste and more sambal for extra kick, if you like. Top with the lime leaves and a squeeze of lime juice and enjoy immediately.

— 100 g (3½ oz) sea salt
— 200 g (7 oz) snake beans
— 150 g (5½ oz) bean sprouts
— 40 g (1½ oz / ¼ cup) finely
   grated roasted coconut
   (see page 92)
— 1 tablespoon Base genep
   (page 50)
— 1 tablespoon Sambal goreng
   (page 75)
— juice of 1 lime
— pinch of Uyah sere (page 71)
   (optional)
— 1 teaspoon sea salt
— ½ teaspoon palm sugar
— pinch of ground white
   pepper (optional)

This is an everyday urab that's popular in home kitchens and restaurants alike – probably because snake beans are so easy to find and prepare. If you're making Nasi bira (page 256) or Nasi yasa (page 253), this is great to serve as an accompaniment. It's bright, hot and sweet, with smoke from the coconut, a hit of freshness from the lime juice and plenty of bite from the sprouts and beans.

URAB KACANG

GREEN BEAN AND BURNT COCONUT SALAD

Bring a small stockpot of water to the boil and add the salt. Add the snake beans and blanch for 8 minutes.

Use tongs to remove the beans from the boiling water, then quickly submerge them in an ice bath to stop them cooking. Strain, place in a bowl and set aside to dry for 10 minutes.

Bring the pot of water to the boil again. Add the bean sprouts and blanch for 4 minutes. Strain, add them to another bowl and set aside to cool.

Cut the green beans into 5 cm (2 in) pieces and set aside.

In a large mixing bowl, combine the blanched beans, bean sprouts and coconut and mix well using your hands. Add the remaining ingredients to the bowl and toss together using your hands, squeezing gently between your fingertips until all of the base is absorbed by the vegetables. Adjust the seasoning if needed and add some white pepper for extra heat, if desired.

Serves 5

- 105 g (3½ oz) sea salt
- 180 g (6½ oz) cassava leaves, stems removed
- 100 g (3½ oz / ½ cup firmly packed) finely grated roasted coconut (see page 92)
- 50 g (1¾ oz) Base genep (page 50)
- 1 tablespoon Sambal goreng (page 75)
- 1 teaspoon lime juice
- pinch of palm sugar
- steamed rice, to serve (for a recipe, see page 111)

Cassava is very common in Bali. It shoots abundantly from the earth in backyard gardens, forests and farms, and even in the grass on the side of the roads. Both the roots and the leaves make it into the paon. Cassava leaves are loved for their grassy, peppery flavour and are often added to urabs like this one.

URAB DON SELA

CASSAVA LEAF AND COCONUT SALAD

Bring a stockpot of water to the boil over a high heat and add 100 grams (3½ oz) of the salt. Turn the heat down to medium, add the cassava leaves and boil for about 10–15 minutes, or until the leaves have wilted and the stems are soft.

Use tongs to remove the leaves from the boiling water and then quickly submerge in an ice bath to stop them cooking.

Using your hands, squeeze any excess water out of the leaves and transfer to a large cutting board.

Roll the leaves into a log and finely chop them. Then, transfer into a large mixing bowl.

Toss the grated coconut and cassava leaves together. Add the base genep, sambal goreng and the remaining salt and toss again. Add the lime juice and sugar and toss some more. Serve with steamed rice or as part of a larger spread.

DRAGONFLIES AND OTHER STRANGE PROTEINS

'You want to find the young dragonflies, the ones that live in the mud. They're called bluwak.' Nyoman Darti, my dear friend and housekeeper, is giving me the lowdown on rice field foraging.

'They have much more flavour. But if they're not in season, adult dragonflies are just as good.'

Nyoman grew up in Payangan, a lush part of the island in the hills just north of Ubud. When she was young, she accompanied her father in the rice fields almost every day, returning home with handfuls of insects, molluscs and other small proteins, which they'd cook together in the paon. Among these delicacies of small paddy-dwelling creatures were the aforementioned bluwak, mature dragonflies, snails, eels and, on rare occasions, land crabs and frogs, which they'd use to make broths, warm salads and steamed, leaf-wrapped meats called tum.

'My father was the best at cooking eel,' Nyoman says. 'He used to chop the meat up with spices and make bakso (meatballs). That was his signature.'

She's telling me all this as we prepare a very special dish together – baby bees brought to my niang (grandmother) as a gift from a friend up north, which we're boiling and massaging with Suna cekuh (page 56) and grated coconut. Bees, which are known locally as nyawan, don't appear on our menu often, but when they do they're a triumph. The young insects are simultaneously sweet and savoury and loaded with clean protein. They taste almost like caramel (and no, they don't sting). We serve them with steamed red rice, Sambal goreng (page 75) and an urab of tabia bun leaves (Javanese long pepper, see page 275) that creep wildly up the coconut trees in our garden.

Nyoman continues telling me about her diet as a child in the village. 'We didn't eat much rice. My father sold most of what we harvested. What we kept, we'd mix with sweet potato to make Nasi sela (page 115).'

This was as recently as thirty-five years ago, when Bali was still morphing into the tourism mammoth it would later become. Native vegetables, roots, fruits and tree leaves were still the main sources of nourishment. Farming and foraging were common practices, supermarkets were few and far between. 'We don't eat like this as often anymore,' Nyoman says. 'This is my favourite kind of food, but it's hard to find the most important ingredient.'

'What's that?' I ask.

'Time.'

Serves 2

- 180 g (6½ oz) fiddlehead
  fern, young tips only,
  woody stems removed
- 1½ tablespoons coconut oil
  (for a recipe, see page 97)
- 1 red (Asian) shallot,
  finely sliced
- 4 garlic cloves, finely sliced
- 1 large red chilli (see
  page 274), sliced
- 2 tabasco chillies, sliced
- 3 teaspoons kecap manis or
  sweet soy sauce (optional)
- pinch of sea salt
- pinch of ground pepper
- ½ teaspoon raw sugar
- Bekakak ayam (page 248),
  to serve
- Tempe manis (page 164),
  to serve
- red, white or yellow rice,
  (see pages 111–12), to serve

Paku (fern tips) are to many paons what spinach might be to a Western kitchen – versatile, reliable everyday greens. They grow wildly in the damp forests, gardens and on the riverbanks of the island's heartlands. You'll also find banana leaf–wrapped bundles of paku at the morning markets – and even in some supermarkets – but the tastiest tips are always freshly foraged.

What's great about fern tips is that they're so sweet, interestingly textured and full of the flavours of the earth, and they don't require a lot of work to prepare. You could use them in ceremonial or everyday salads, such as lawar (see page 240) or urab (see page 132), but you can also just toss them in a pan with garlic, chilli and some red (Asian) shallots. Some cooks add kecap manis for extra sweetness, while others prefer to let the flavour of the coconut oil sing through. We suggest serving them with bekakak ayam, tempe manis and red, white or yellow rice.

PAKU TUMIS

YOUNG FIDDLEHEAD FERN TIPS WITH GARLIC, CHILLIES AND SHALLOTS

Wash and rinse the fern tips well, then spin them in a salad spinner or drain them in a colander. The drier the tips, the better they will cook, so it's also worth the extra step of laying them on a tray lined with paper towel to soak up any lingering moisture. Set aside.

Heat a wok over a high heat and add the oil. When the oil is hot, add the shallot, garlic and chilli and sauté for 5 minutes, or until fragrant. Add the fern tips and continue to sauté for 6–8 minutes, or until the fern tips have wilted.

Add the kecap manis, if using, and stir, then add the salt, pepper and sugar and give it another stir.

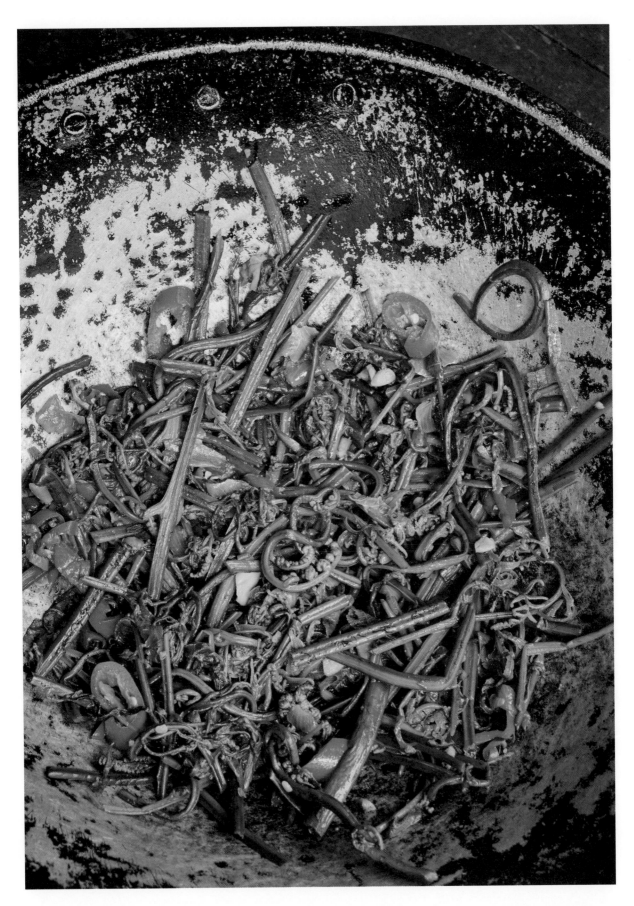

Serves 4

- 2 banana blossoms, red outer petals and stems removed, finely sliced
- 1 tablespoon sea salt, plus extra, to season
- 250 g (9 oz/1½ cups) finely grated roasted coconut (see page 92)
- 90 g (3 oz/½ cup) Sambal goreng (page 75), plus extra, to serve
- juice of ½ small lime
- steamed rice (for a recipe, see page 111), to serve

'There are several varieties of banana trees growing in my grandmother's garden. There's a couple of dang saba trees that produce a starchy fruit that's great for cooking with, and some pisang kayu trees that grow narrow green bananas that we often use for offerings. The majority, however, are pisang batu trees that grow short, flat-sided fruits with stone-riddled centres. We don't often eat them, but we do eat the fat, sweet blossoms, which are perfect for serving as vegetables. When properly cooked, pusuh (banana blossom) takes on a sort of meatiness. Texturally, it feels a little bit like cooked artichoke. In this recipe, the banana blossom takes on the smokiness of the roasted coconut and the sweetness of the sambal goreng, and ends up tasting kind of like bacon. I love it because it embodies the real root-to-fruit philosophy of traditional Balinese cooking, which at its purest is really more about plants than protein.'

— Maya

URAB PUSUH

BANANA BLOSSOM AND COCONUT SALAD

Bring a large saucepan of water to the boil.

Meanwhile, add the banana blossoms to a large mixing bowl and break them up with your fingers. Give them a good toss and add 1 tablespoon of sea salt to help extract the bitter sap.

Once the water has reached a lively boil, throw the banana blossoms in and boil, covered, for 4 minutes, or until they're soft but with a bit of bite. Strain and let them cool under running water for about 1 minute. Transfer to a medium mixing bowl, then set aside.

Add the coconut to the banana blossoms and toss well using your hands. Add the sambal goreng and lime juice and sea salt, to taste. Toss again, making sure everything is well combined.

Serve with steamed rice and extra sambal goreng on the side.

Serves 4

- 100 ml (3½ fl oz) coconut oil (for a recipe, see page 97)
- 110 g (4 oz) plain soybean tempe, cut into 2 cm (¾ in) cubes or triangles
- 2 garlic cloves, finely sliced
- 1 red (Asian) shallot, finely sliced
- 2–3 tabasco chillies, finely sliced (optional)
- 2 tomatoes, sliced
- 1 teaspoon sea salt
- 6 spring onions (scallions), diced

'This tempe, or tempeh, recipe is simple but powerful. My niang (grandmother) eats it almost every day. It's a true testament to the magic that can happen when garlic, red (Asian) shallots, tomatoes and good coconut oil join forces. It works nicely on its own with steamed rice or as a side in a family-style spread. You could add a sliced chilli or two for extra spice, but it's just as nice without the burn. I add or omit chillies depending on my mood.'

– Maya

TEMPE BUMBU TOMAT
TEMPE WITH TOMATO, GARLIC AND SHALLOTS

Heat the coconut oil in a wok over a high heat. Carefully add the tempe and fry it for 2 minutes on each side, or until golden-brown and with crisp edges.

Remove the tempe from the wok using a spider ladle or slotted spoon and place it on a plate lined with paper towel to soak up any excess oil.

Using the same wok and oil, add the garlic, shallot and chilli, if using, and fry for 20 seconds, or until caramelised. Add the tomatoes and salt and cook, stirring, for about 2 minutes, or until the tomatoes have released their juices.

Add the tempe back into the wok and stir well. Add the spring onion and stir again. Cook for 2 minutes and transfer everything, oil and all, into a bowl. Serve immediately.

Makes 10

- 10 eggs, hard-boiled and peeled
- 8 tablespoons Base genep (page 50)
- 3 salam leaves
- 450 ml (15 fl oz) water

'These spiced eggs are a main feature on most daily household menus. They also make their way into lots of warungs (local eateries) and buffet spreads on special occasions. In fact, it's hard for me to imagine a complete meal without them. I love how the egg whites absorb the colours and flavours of the spices and how the sauce becomes thick and caramelised, just asking to be soaked up by a side of steamed rice.'

– Maya

TALUH MEPINDANG

SPICED EGGS

Place all the ingredients in a medium saucepan, cover and bring to the boil over a high heat.

Reduce the heat to low and let it simmer for 20–30 minutes, or until the liquid has reduced by half.

Place the eggs on a serving platter, either whole or cut into halves, and spoon the sauce over the top.

Serves 6

- 1 kg (2 lb 3 oz) chicken breast
- 2 tablespoons Air kunyit
  (page 70)
- 125 ml (4 fl oz / ½ cup)
  Santen (coconut milk,
  page 94)
- 1 salam leaf
- 3 tablespoons Suna cekuh
  (page 56), uncooked
- 255 ml (9 fl oz) coconut oil
  (for a recipe, see page 97)
- 6 red (Asian) shallots, finely
  sliced
- 1 teaspoon shrimp paste
- 1 teaspoon salt
- 250 g (8½ oz / 1½ cups) finely
  grated roasted coconut (see
  page 92)
- 3 tablespoons Sambal goreng
  (page 75)
- ½ lime, to serve
- steamed rice (for a recipe,
  see page 111), to serve
- urab of your choice
  (pages 132–5, 204), to serve

Tip

This recipe also works well
with grilled or roasted chicken.

'This dish was one of my grandfather's favourites. "He didn't eat meat often," my niang (grandmother) said, "he would cook a duck once a month and drink its raw blood to preserve his strength."

When chicken was on the menu (which was a rare occasion in those days) he would often request this dish. There's something inherently tender about gecok – it might be from the way the coconut milk is massaged into the bird or how the smokiness of the roasted coconut follows through on the palate after the buzz from the sambal subsides. For me, it's a shining example of the sophistication of old-fashioned Balinese cooking and how every step comes together to create harmony on the plate.'

– Maya

GECOK

SHREDDED COCONUT-TURMERIC CHICKEN

Add the chicken and turmeric water to a large mixing bowl and massage the meat well with the liquid. Set aside.

In a medium saucepan, simmer the coconut milk and salam leaf over a low heat. Add one teaspoon of suna cekuh and bring to the boil. Once it's reached a lively boil, remove from the heat and set aside to cool.

Heat 200 ml (7 fl oz) of the oil in a large wok over a high heat and fry the chicken for about 4 minutes, or until nice and evenly caramelised on both sides and cooked through. Remove the chicken from the wok and place it on paper towel to soak up any excess oil. Let it rest and cool.

Once the chicken has cooled, roughly tear the meat into strips using your fingers – you want it to be nicely shredded but not too stringy. Set aside.

Heat another 5 tablespoons of oil in the wok and fry the shallots, stirring regularly so they don't burn, for 4 minutes, or until golden. Remove the shallot from the wok with a spider ladle or slotted spoon and set aside on a plate lined with paper towel to soak up excess oil.

In the same hot oil, sauté the remaining suna cekuh for 2 minutes, or until fragrant. Pour the suna cekuh – oil and all – into a bowl and set aside.

Gently fry the shrimp paste in the wok for around 1 minute, or until pungent, and place in a small bowl to cool. Once it's cool enough to handle, add the salt and use your hand to massage it into the shrimp paste. Set aside.

In a large mixing bowl, toss the coconut, chicken, suna cekuh, shallot and shrimp paste mixture together using your hands.

Slowly pour in the coconut milk a little at a time until the chicken is evenly coated but not swimming in liquid. Add the sambal goreng and toss again. Squeeze the lime over the top and add another pinch of sambal goreng, if desired. Serve with steamed rice and an urab of your choice.

Serves 8

- 1.2 kg (2 lb 10 oz) young
  jackfruit, peeled and cut into
  3 cm (1¼ in) cubes
- 100 g (3½ oz) dry red beans,
  soaked for an hour
- 4 tablespoons coconut oil
  (for a recipe, see page 97)
- 300 g (10½ oz/1 cup) Base
  genep (page 50)
- 1 chicken carcass, roughly
  chopped
- 3 salam leaves, roughly torn
- 1.5 litres (51 fl oz/6 cups)
  water or vegetable stock
  (for a recipe, see page 72)
- 2 tablespoons sea salt
  (see Tip)
- steamed rice (for a recipe,
  see page 111), to serve

In Bali young jackfruit is often eaten as a savoury food. It's the ultimate meat substitute that becomes pink, fleshy and tender when it's slow-cooked and adequately spiced. This particular stew isn't strictly vegetarian, but you can omit the chicken bones and replace the water with vegetable stock if you'd like it to be. It's usually served as a side but works just as well on its own with rice.

JUKUT NANGKA

YOUNG JACKFRUIT STEW

Boil the jackfruit in a large stockpot of water over a high heat for 20 minutes, or until it becomes soft enough to poke with a fork. Strain and set aside.

Meanwhile, boil the beans for around 20 minutes, strain and set aside.

Heat the oil in a large stockpot and sauté the base genep until fragrant. Add the chicken bones, jackfruit and salam leaves and stir well. Add the red beans and stir again.

Add the water or stock and salt and bring to the boil over a high heat. Lower the heat to medium–low, cover and let simmer for 30 minutes, or until the jackfruit is dark and tender – it should be brown on the outside, pink on the inside and soft enough to pull apart with a fork. Season to taste.

Serve in a large bowl with kuah (broth) as part of a larger spread, or on its own with steamed rice.

Tip

Store-bought stocks often contain a lot of salt, so if that's what you're using, start by adding half the amount of salt, then season to taste.

Serves 4

- 250 g (9 oz) boneless chicken thighs, skin-on
- 4 heaped tablespoons Sambal matah (page 76)
- 1 torch ginger flower, finely sliced (optional)
- 2 tablespoons coconut oil (for a recipe, see page 97)
- sea salt, to taste
- 4 lime leaves, finely sliced
- juice of 1 small lime

This recipe is a great way to jazz up leftover roast chicken. It's usually served as a condiment alongside steamed rice, vegetables and even other meats – a bulked-up sambal, if you like. In some parts of the island, kecicang (torch ginger flowers, see page 277) are sometimes tossed through, too. These magenta treasures are punchy, aromatic and extremely unique in flavour. If you can get your hands on fresh flowers, slice them up super finely and throw them in.

AYAM SISIT

SHREDDED CHICKEN WITH RAW SAMBAL

Preheat a grill or charcoal barbecue to a high heat.

Season the chicken with salt and black pepper. Place on the hot grill or barbecue and cook for 8 minutes. Turn over the chicken and cook for an additional 5–7 minutes, or until golden and cooked through.

Pull the chicken apart using your fingers and roughly tear the meat and skin.

Place the chicken in a medium mixing bowl and toss through a handful of sambal matah and the torch ginger flower, if using, adding a glug (no more than a tablespoon) of oil if the mixture seems dry. There should be an even ratio of chicken to sambal, so add more if needed. Season with salt to taste and garnish with the lime leaves and the lime juice.

Tum parcels are usually made from duck, chicken, pork or buffalo offcuts marinated in base rajang and steamed in banana leaves folded to resemble the great Mount Agung. Different variations appear during festival times, family gatherings and temple feasts. We've seen them wrapped in cacao leaves in central Bali, which made them a touch drier and more fragrant. Some cooks add the blood of whatever animal they've just butchered for sweetness and flavour – a Balinese black pudding of sorts. Others omit meat altogether and use tofu, tempe or even oyster mushrooms instead. When you unfold them, they're kind of like steamed, spiced meatballs – rich, complex and smoky if you've steamed them over a wood fire.

The level of seasoning is very personal – you may or may not want to include sugar and you might want to add more salt. If you'd like to check the seasoning before you wrap and steam the parcels, do a meatball test (see Tip).

To wrap each parcel, add a small handful of meat in the centre of the leaves.

To fold, hold one side of the leaves in one hand and fold in one of the corners with the other.

Fold in the remaining corners.

It should look like a little pouch.

Wrap a strip of banana leaf around the parcel.

Fasten the ends with a toothpick.

- 12 banana leaves
  (20 × 13 cm/8 x 5 in)
- toothpicks

- 250 g (9 oz) minced duck
  (or use chicken mince if you
  can't find duck)
- 50 g (1¾ oz) duck or chicken
  hearts, chopped
- 1 shallot, finely chopped
- 8 garlic cloves, finely
  chopped
- 2 tabasco chillies, finely
  chopped
- 140 g (5 oz/⅓ cup) Base
  rajang (page 53)
- 1 teaspoon Uyah sere
  (page 71)
- 2 tablespoons coconut oil
  (for a recipe, see page 97)
- ½ tablespoon sea salt
  (optional)
- 1 teaspoon palm sugar
  (optional)
- steamed rice (for a recipe,
  see page 111), to serve
- Sambal goreng (page 75),
  to serve

Tip

To test the seasoning, heat
2 tablespoons of oil in a sauté
pan over a medium heat for
2 minutes, or until smoke point.
Make a tiny meatball the size
of a hazelnut and fry it in the
oil for 3–4 minutes, or until
cooked through. Taste and
decide what seasoning you
need to adjust – add more base
if it's too bland, or more salt
and pepper if needed.

TUM BEBEK

STEAMED DUCK PARCELS

In a large bowl, mix the minced duck with the hearts. Set aside.

In a separate bowl, combine the shallot, garlic, chilli, base rajang and uyah sere.

Heat the oil in a small saucepan over a medium heat for 3 minutes until just warm, then take it off the heat and let cool until cool enough to handle.

Pour the oil over the shallot mixture and give it a good toss using your hands.

Add the meat, and salt and sugar, if using. Using your hands, mix everything together until well combined. Set aside. You can chill the spiced meat in the fridge for 20–30 minutes to make it easier to shape and wrap.

Prepare the banana leaves for wrapping (see page 27) and use the guide opposite to wrap the filling in the banana leaves.

Fill a steamer pot with water to about 2.5 cm (1 in) below the steaming rack. Bring the water to the boil and cover to let the steam build up inside, about 10 minutes. Place the parcels in the steamer pot and steam for 15 minutes. Remove the parcels from the pot and serve warm, unwrapped, with rice and sambal goreng.

MAGIC IN HER FINGERTIPS

My niang (grandmother) and I are making urab in the paon. I'm grating the last of the coconut, and she's sorting through the cassava leaves, picking the youngest and palest of the bunch. She's undressed from the waist up, cooling down after a morning of gardening.

'Is it true you have magic in your fingertips?' I ask.

She laughs, her eyes disappearing into the mess of wrinkles around her cheekbones and above her brow. 'These hands of mine don't use magic, they use resilience,' she says. 'I've cooked through the Dutch, the Japanese, when the volcano erupted, even through heartache.'

We blanch the leaves and she moves across the room to the cupboard, returning with a plate of sambal goreng. I strain the greens, roll them into cylinders and chop them into even slivers. My niang takes a handful and places them in a large bowl. 'I'll mix,' she says.

I decide to pry. 'I thought you said you'd never been in love,' I inquire, as I watch the caramelised shallots, garlic, grated coconut and cassava leaves amalgamate between her strong fingers.

She appears to ignore me, lifting her right hand up towards her nose and closing her eyes. She's checking the seasoning. 'Needs salt.'

Just as I go to change the topic she rolls into another fit of laughter, this one so robust that her eyes begin to stream. 'You try being married to a man with more than one wife,' she says.

Keplus, her assistant of more than thirty years, giggles and shakes her head over by the stove. The humour is infectious and we all end up cackling and smiling and slapping our thighs in amusement.

The urab is ready. We spread it out over a plate lined with banana leaves and finish it with a squeeze of lime. 'Now you can taste,' my niang says. It's smoky and vibrant with a touch more salt than usual – extra seasoning, perhaps, by way of our happy tears.

- 100 ml (3½ fl oz) coconut oil (for a recipe, see page 97)
- 450 g (1 lb/1¾ cups) Base rajang (page 53)
- ½ tablespoon Uyah sere (page 71)
- 10 salam leaves
- 5 lemongrass stems, white part only, crushed (see page 28)
- 2½ cm (1 in) piece fresh ginger, sliced
- 3½ cm (1½ in) piece fresh galangal, sliced
- 6 tabasco chillies, halved lengthways
- ½ tablespoon ground black pepper
- ½ tablespoon ground coriander
- ½ tablespoon salt
- 1½ tablespoons palm sugar
- 2.5 litres (85 fl oz/10 cups) chicken stock (for a recipe, see page 73)
- 1 kg (2 lb 3 oz) pork belly, tough skin layer removed and cut into four equal square pieces
- 500 g (1 lb 2 oz) pork neck, cut into four equal pieces
- steamed rice (for a recipe, see page 111), to serve
- Lawar kacang (page 243), to serve
- Sambal mbe (page 78), to serve

Babi genyol is pork braised slowly with base rajang. Genyol means to jiggle in Balinese, so the name of this dish reveals exactly what it is: pork that is fatty and jiggles in a dark, rich sauce. We've recommended using pork neck and belly for this recipe, but cheek works well, too.

BABI GENYOL
SLOW-BRAISED SPICED PORK

Heat the oil in a large pot or rondeau pan over a medium heat for 3–4 minutes. Add the base rajang, uyah sere and salam leaves, and sauté for 3 minutes, stirring continuously to prevent the spices from burning.

Add the lemongrass, ginger, galangal and chilli to the pan and sauté for 1–2 minutes, or until fragrant.

Add the pepper, coriander, salt, palm sugar and chicken stock, turn the heat up to high and bring to the boil.

Once boiling, add the pork, cover with a lid or aluminium foil and reduce the heat to low. Cook for 3 hours, or until the meat is tender.

Remove the pork from the pan and place in a serving bowl, keeping the sauce in the pan.

To serve, slice the meat into 3 cm (1¼ in) cubes and spoon the sauce over the top. Best served with steamed rice, lawar kacang and sambal mbe on the side.

Serves 2–4

– 4 small taro roots, (approx.
   150–160 g/5½–6 oz each),
   unpeeled
– ½ teaspoon sea salt
– 4 tablespoons Gula Bali
   (page 98)

'This is a very straightforward dish – just roasted taro with a dash of sea salt and gula Bali. Some cooks like to add grated coconut, but we prefer to keep it super simple. At home, we often have keladi metambus for breakfast or with our afternoon coffee. In some rural parts of central Bali it's served as a temple snack before or after prayers. It's a strong example of uncomplicated Balinese cooking – a handful of natural ingredients and a good roaring fire, and you've got a humble, healthy snack from the earth.'

– Maya

KELADI
METAMBUS
ROASTED TARO

Start by preparing a wood fire or charcoal grill. A barbecue will also work but a wood fire is best.

Once the fire is rolling and there's plenty of hot coals, simply bury the taro underneath the coals. Cover them completely to make sure they cook evenly, and cook for 20 minutes. If you're using a grill, you'll need to turn them. You could also wrap them in aluminium foil, but you won't get the same smoky, charred result.

Remove the taro from the fire and pierce them with a fork or sharp stick. If you can do this with ease, they're ready. If the centre is still hard, let them cook a while longer. Set aside for about 15 minutes, or until cool enough to handle.

Peel off the charred skins and cut each root into thick slices.

Place the sliced taro on a large plate or platter and add the salt and a generous swirl of gula Bali. Serve with tea or coffee.

Serves 6

- 175 g (6 oz) palm sugar,
  finely chopped or grated
- 2 bird's eye chillies,
  roughly crushed in a mortar
  and pestle
- 1 heaped tablespoon
  tamarind pulp
- 2 teaspoons sea salt
- 100 ml (3½ fl oz) water
- 3 jicamas, finely sliced

'This is a really quick rujak. The jicama is cool and fresh, and pops nicely against the sweet, hot, tangy sauce. We haven't included terasi (shrimp paste), but you could throw in a teaspoon for a more pungent dressing. This recipe calls for two chillies, which provides a nice consistent buzz – use one for less heat. Slice the jicama as finely as possible for the most delicious results.'

– Maya

RUJAK BENGKUANG

JICAMA RUJAK

Combine the palm sugar, chilli, tamarind and salt in a mixing bowl, and, using your hands, squeeze them together until they form a rough paste. You'll need to give the chillies a little extra attention to make sure they break down completely. Remember not to touch your eyes.

Add the water, a bit at a time, and keep massaging the ingredients together until all the sugar chunks and tamarind have dissolved and a watery sauce has formed.

Add the jicama and lightly toss it through the sauce until all the jicama has been dressed, being careful not to bruise the jicama too much.

Serves 4

- 150 ml (5 fl oz) coconut oil
  (for a recipe, see page 97)
- 600 g (1 lb 5 oz) plain
  soybean tempe, cut into 1 cm
  (½ in) cubes
- 2 small red (Asian) shallots,
  sliced
- 2 garlic cloves, sliced
- 2 large red chillies, seeded
  and finely sliced
- 4 tablespoons Tempe manis
  sauce (recipe below)
- 120 g (4½ oz / ½ cup) Sambal
  tomat (page 84)

TEMPE MANIS SAUCE
- 150 ml (5 fl oz) water at room
  temperature
- 125 g (4½ oz) chopped palm
  sugar or granulated coconut
  sugar
- 2½ tablespoons kecap manis
  or sweet soy sauce

Tempe, or tempeh, is originally from Java, but it has become such a big part of our modern culinary make-up that we decided to include it. The fermented beans, which are fashioned into cakes, wrapped in banana leaf and sold at the markets, have an earthiness about them and a density that makes them perfect for braising in curries, frying in thick slices as a snack or cut into small batons and tossed through rice and noodles. This recipe for tempe tossed through a palm sugar sauce is an Indonesian staple. It's quick, comforting and good for you. Buy the best-quality organic tempe you can find.

TEMPE MANIS
SWEET AND SALTY TEMPE

Heat the oil in a wok over a medium heat to 145°C (290°F), or until it reaches smoke point.

Slowly drop the tempe into the wok and fry for 10–15 minutes, or until crispy and golden-brown.

Remove the tempe from the wok using a spider ladle or slotted spoon and transfer to a tray lined with paper towel. Set aside and reserve the oil for later.

To make the sauce, combine all the ingredients in a small saucepan and simmer, stirring occasionally, over a medium heat for 15–20 minutes, or until the liquid has reduced by 25 per cent and the sauce is thick and dark.

Reheat 3 tablespoons of the reserved oil and sauté the shallots, garlic and chilli for 3–4 minutes, or until fragrant and the chilli has wilted.

Add the fried tempe and the sauce and cook, stirring, for 1–2 minutes.

Add the sambal tomat and stir well to combine.

Serves 10

- 170 g (6 oz) palm sugar, finely chopped or grated
- 4–5 bird's eye chillies, roughly crushed in a mortar and pestle
- 1 heaped tablespoon sea salt
- 135 g (5 oz) tamarind pulp
- 100 ml (3½ fl oz) filtered water
- ½ teaspoon shrimp paste, rolled into a ball
- 480 g (1 lb 1 oz / 2 cups) soursop (see page 277), seeds removed, flesh roughly torn
- 380 g (13½ oz) pineapple, finely sliced
- 175 g (6 oz) rambutans, seeds removed, flesh roughly torn

'This rujak reminds me of downtime, family gatherings, dinner parties and hot, lazy afternoons. It comes courtesy of our housekeeper, Nyoman, who is an avid rujak consumer herself. We often make and eat it together. She likes hers super spicy, but I prefer to turn down the heat, letting the tamarind sing a little louder. What's fun about this recipe is that it's such an adventure on the palate. The sauce is sweet, tangy, spicy and a little bit savoury from the salt and terasi (shrimp paste). The soursop is soft and complex, the pineapple bright and textural and the rambutans bring sweetness. When all the elements join forces the result is big, exciting and refreshing. It's a really fun dessert. If you can't source soursop and rambutans, swap them for jicama, mango or pomelo.'
— *Maya*

NYOMAN'S RUJAK

FRESH FRUIT WITH TAMARIND DRESSING

In a mixing bowl, combine the sugar, chilli and salt by hand, using your fingers to gently crush the palm sugar to remove any chunks. Add the tamarind and repeat the process until all the ingredients are well combined.

Add half of the water and keep mixing, using your hands, until the ingredients form a thick sauce.

Add the shrimp paste and the remaining water and mix again.

Toss all the fruit through the dressing using your hands. Portion into individual bowls and serve as a snack or dessert.

Serves 4

- 250 g (9 oz) black rice, soaked overnight
- 2 pandan leaves
- 1.2 litres (41 fl oz) water
- 100 g (3½ oz / ½ cup) palm sugar, roughly chopped
- pinch of sea salt
- 350 ml (12 fl oz) Santen (coconut milk, page 94)
- 100 g (3½ oz) ripe jackfruit, finely chopped

For many of us, this sweet, rich and warm rice pudding was one of our earliest foods. Most Balinese cooks will cook the rice in the coconut cream, while others will pour it over separately at the end – this recipe does a bit of both.

BUBUR INJIN

SWEET BLACK RICE PUDDING

Rinse and strain the soaked rice.

In a large saucepan, add the rice, pandan leaves and water and bring to the boil over a high heat. Reduce the heat to low and simmer, stirring occasionally, for 30 minutes, or until the water has reduced and the rice releases a sweet, grassy aroma.

Add the palm sugar and a generous pinch of salt and cook, stirring, until the sugar has dissolved completely.

Pour in 300 ml (10 fl oz) of the coconut milk and cook for a further minute.

Serve warm with jackfruit and the remaining coconut milk to pour over the pudding.

Serves 4

- 2 pandan leaves
- 280 g (10 oz) plain (all-purpose) flour
- 1 teaspoon limestone paste (see page 275)
- 2 teaspoons sea salt
- 3 saba bananas (see page 273), thickly sliced
- 110 g (4 oz) fresh mature coconut, finely grated
- Gula Bali (page 98), to serve

'In the late afternoon, after his daily nap, my father sits on his balcony with a cup of coffee and something sweet, and pisang rai is one of his favourite treats. You could describe it as a lighter take on fried banana, minus the oil. The bananas are cut into chunks, battered and boiled, then brightened with powdery grated coconut and a good drizzle of palm sugar syrup. It's a nourishing, warming and gently sweetened dish that works just as well for breakfast as it does for dessert.'

– Maya

PISANG RAI

BOILED BANANAS WITH GRATED COCONUT

Place the pandan leaves and 2 litres (68 fl oz/8 cups) water in a large saucepan over a high heat. Cover and bring to the boil.

Meanwhile, combine the flour and 300 ml (10 fl oz) water in a medium mixing bowl and work into a batter using your hands. Once a thick batter has formed, set aside.

Combine the limestone paste with a splash of water in a small bowl, crushing it between your fingers to help it dissolve. Pour it into the batter and mix well. Add the salt and mix again, then toss the bananas through the batter using your hands.

Using a tablespoon, scoop the banana slices out of the batter, one piece at a time, tilting the spoon a little to pour off any excess batter. Drop the banana pieces into the boiling water. Cook for about 5 minutes, or until they float to the top and the batter has become opaque – the fruit should be just visible in the centre.

Remove the banana from the water with a spider ladle or slotted spoon and place on a serving dish. Let cool for about 5 minutes.

Sprinkle a few tablespoons of coconut over the top, keeping the rest in a small bowl to serve. Serve with gula Bali or granulated coconut sugar and a cup of strong, steaming coffee.

FROM
THE SEA

–

FROM
THE SEA

–

FROM
THE SEA

–

FROM
THE SEA

–

FROM
THE SEA

–

FROM
THE SEA

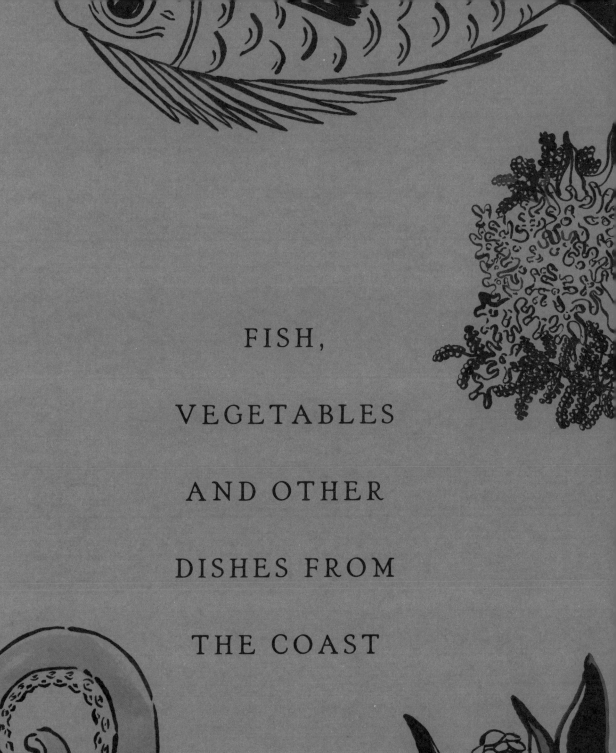

FISH,

VEGETABLES

AND OTHER

DISHES FROM

THE COAST

WHERE
RICE
DOESN'T
GROW

On Nusa Penida, food is survival. Even though it's geographically very close to Bali, it's arid, rocky limestone and nowhere near as fertile. In fact, Nusa Penida is a dry island, without lakes or rivers, and people depend on rainwater to farm. This means we cannot grow rice on the island, and corn and cassava replace rice as our main starch. Seafood is a staple for daily meals, often served with undis (pigeon peas), black beans, red beans, lima beans or fresh young pretzel beans for vegetables. Before cargo boats started delivering food from the mainland, our diet was entirely based on what nature could offer. It's no exaggeration to say that when I was growing up, our lives revolved around growing, catching and preserving food. If you didn't have a routine, you might go to bed hungry.

In my village of Banjar Nyuh, most people were fishermen or seaweed farmers. In my family, we did both because our house was on the beach. Seaweed farming and fishing are often tandem labours because the schedules needed to carry out the work are opposites. Fishing needs high tides and seaweed farming needs low tides. We would go out to fish in the pre-dawn hours around four or five o'clock in the morning, return by eight am to take a rest, then set out to work on our seaweed plots at low tide around midday. Then it was back out to sea in the evenings after we had eaten our supper, fishing in the dark of night at high tide for another few hours. Fishing is seasonal, which is another reason to farm seaweed, as it can provide an income year-round.

When we did fish, we fished to find food, not for leisure, but it still brought me so much joy. The sea around Nusa Penida is wild and unruly but full of bounty – tuna, red snapper, trevally, grouper, garfish, mackerel, sea eel, squid and octopus. The latter was my favourite. My father taught me how to catch octopus in the tide pools after sunset with just a lantern and a hand-held net or spear. We'd chop the octopus into small pieces, massage it with Suna cekuh (page 56) and grill it over a wood fire. We'd dress up the fish we caught with Sambal tomat (page 84), and the heads and bones were slow-cooked into stocks or soups.

A lot of our time was spent at sea. When my father was still a fisherman, he used to go out on a wooden jukung (outrigger canoe). The Badung Strait can be perilous and this was dangerous work, so I didn't start fishing until boats with engines were introduced to the island when I was about ten years old. Since my dad's boat didn't have an engine, I learned to fish from our neighbours Pak Pas and Pak Su. Our legs served as fishing poles – we used to tie the end of the line around one thigh and threw the other end into the sea behind the jukung as it moved slowly through the water. The line stretched for 40 metres (130 feet) and had multiple hooks spaced out around two metres (6.5 feet) from each other. We'd wait, sometimes for hours. When we felt a tugging sensation, we knew we'd caught a fish, so we'd slow the boat in the hopes of hooking a few more fish. I, of course, was a lot smaller than my adult companions, so when the line became too heavy to bear, I'd reel it in and unhook the fish one by one, trying not to slice open my hands or legs on the sharp hooks in the process.

One of my strongest childhood memories was when Pak Su let me steer the engine on his fishing boat for the first time when I was thirteen years old. I only drove the boat along the shoreline and near the mangroves during the midday daylight, but it was exhilarating all the same. The reason we would go out to sea at different times of the day was to catch different types of fish. In daylight, we would throw our fishing lines into the sea in the hopes that yellowfin tuna or skipjack tuna would bite. In the dark of night, we used nets to catch the fish that swam in schools, such as blue mackerel and garfish. Tongkol baby tuna was caught in nets just before the sunrise, when the fish would swim to the surface to find food. By the time I was in high school, my body was strong enough to handle the boat and fishing nets by myself, so I became a full-time fisherman when I was sixteen years old. Fishing meant going to work every day at 4 o'clock in the morning. From my house on the beach, I was constantly looking at the ocean and watching the currents, thinking of what fish I could catch where.

Because I was always thinking of how I could put food on the table for my family, fishing was more important than attending school, or so I thought at the time. I could never make the connection as to how a certificate was going to feed my family. I've always learned by doing, and fishing had immediate, tangible results. School was impractical and unnecessary, I thought, and I used to believe it was a waste of my time. After all, I had a family of twelve that needed taking care of, and I was the eldest son. I was usually late to school after fishing in the early mornings, and I would often fall asleep in class because I had been awake since 4 am. Looking back now, I was lucky to graduate.

Top left: Wayan's aunt makes a traditional sweet known as jaja bindu.
Top right: Pounding rice into flour using a traditional lu and lesung.
Bottom: Lunch preparations – cucumbers and sweet potato.

On Nusa Penida, our daily routine of gathering food changed with the seasons. During the rainy months from December through to February, food was fresh. My grandfather, grandmother and uncle lived in the hills where they grew cassava, corn and beans. My mother and father lived on the coast and grew seaweed and caught fish. So, as a family we'd exchange harvests. We'd stew the cassava roots, ears of corn and beans, a little bit like a bubuh (porridge) called ledok-ledok. Our protein came from grilled or fried fish seasoned with base. If we were lucky, we'd have fresh bayam (kelor leaves), green papaya or cassava leaves for vegetables.

In the wet season, we'd grow and harvest more than we could eat to prepare for the drier months to come. When the monsoon ends, not a single drop of rain touches Nusa Penida for about six months, so our focus shifts from collecting food to collecting water – a different but significant form of survival mode. We pound our corn and cassava stores into what might be described as a chunky polenta that we boil into a porridge with beans or fish. My grandmother kept our excess corn on a bamboo rack above the stove called a penapi. The smoke from the fire would dry the corn and keep pests at bay. All my life, I've never had an insect in my corn, and that's without a jar or a fridge or a cupboard in sight.

Meat, as you can imagine, was a rarity. We probably ate it every six months. We raised every animal ourselves and reserved them for celebrations such as Galungan, when our whole family would come home to pray and feast on free-range kampung chickens and spiced and spit-roasted black Balinese pigs.

Now that I think of it, it was precisely the daily routines of fishing and farming throughout my childhood on Nusa Penida that prepared me for a professional life as a chef: there is a lot of prep, physical labour and exhaustion, all for a fleeting moment of temporary reward (or no reward at all if the dish burns, the crop fails or the fish don't bite). Likewise, every day is an opportunity for something new, a challenge or a reward. Working as a chef is an unpredictable career. One must surrender to the obstacles and overcome them moment-by-moment. Being a chef, a fisherman or a farmer requires a person to either adapt or quit; it is a career dependent on the seasons, daily weather patterns – many variables out of our immediate control, and the consequences are immediate. Then we pick ourselves up and start the effort all over again the next day.

I hope you enjoy these traditional Balinese seafood recipes we've gathered for you in this chapter. In both catching and preparing food, the sea has always been my speciality. Although there was a time I was jaded by the idea of seafood when I was eating it every day as a child, today I look back on those days with fondness. We ate simply but well, and we savoured every bite – as one must do on an island where rice doesn't grow.

Makes 1.5 kg (3 lb 5 oz)

- 500 g (1 lb 2 oz) white rice
- 2 cassava roots (approx. 500 g/1 lb 2 oz), peeled, soaked for 10 minutes and coarsely grated
- ½ teaspoon sea salt

'Cassava plays a big role in life on Nusa Penida, and in other arid parts of the main island. I grew up eating it and have many memories of my mother and grandmother cooking with both the roots and leaves in sweet and savoury dishes alike. This recipe is made from grated cassava, which makes for a wonderful, nutrient-rich rice substitute. It reminds me of a time when most of the families on our small island grew their own food – corn, beans, sorghum, squash and, of course, cassava – and sun-dried it to use sparingly throughout the year. Sometimes, we'd eat cassava plain, and other times we combined it with whatever rice we had. The little slivers of cassava bring a lovely sweetness to the grains and take a small handful of rice so much further.'

— *Wayan*

NASI SELA GAYOT

CASSAVA RICE

Rinse the rice under running tap water in a large strainer until the water runs almost clear. Transfer the rinsed rice into a large mixing bowl, cover it with water and leave to soak for about 15 minutes.

Meanwhile, fill a medium or large steamer pot with water and bring to the boil. The water level should be 2½ cm (1 in) below the centre steam rack.

Strain the rice and transfer it to the steamer pot. Cover with a lid and steam the rice for about 15 minutes.

Soak the grated cassava in water for 10 minutes, then strain and squeeze out any excess water using your hands. Set aside.

Remove the rice from the steamer and place it in a medium stainless steel bowl. Add the cassava and salt, stir using a wooden spoon, then pour over hot water from the steamer pot to just cover. Stir again, cover and let the mixture steep for about 20 minutes.

Meanwhile, fill the steamer pot with water to about 2½ cm (1 in) below the steamer basket and slowly bring to the boil over a low heat.

Give the steeped rice and cassava a stir to loosen the grains, then return to the steamer. Turn the heat up to medium, cover and steam for a further 20 minutes.

Serves 5

- 2 tablespoons vegetable oil, plus extra for deep-frying (about 200 ml/7 fl oz)
- 1–2 red (Asian) shallots, finely sliced
- 4 garlic cloves, finely sliced
- 1 × 350 g (12½ oz) skinless tuna fillet
- 140 g (5 oz/½ cup) Base genep (page 50)
- 80 ml (2½ fl oz/⅓ cup) Santen (coconut milk, page 94)
- 2 lime leaves
- 2 tablespoons granulated palm sugar
- 1 teaspoon shrimp paste
- ½ teaspoon sea salt
- Sambal tomat (page 84), to serve

Pulung pulung are deep-fried meatballs. They can be made from chicken, pork and even mashed cassava, but in the coastal areas they're almost always made from fish – mackerel, to be specific, or baby tuna when in season. They're sweet and aromatic from the santen (coconut milk) and lime leaves, and make for moreish little savoury snacks, starters or condiments with rice – just add sambal.

PULUNG PULUNG

FRIED FISH BALLS

Heat the oil in a small sauté pan over a medium heat and cook the shallots and garlic for about 4 minutes, stirring continuously, until fragrant and translucent. Set aside.

Use a cleaver to mince the fresh tuna and place it in a large mixing bowl. Add the base genep, coconut milk, lime leaves, shallot, garlic, sugar, shrimp paste and salt and use your hands to massage everything well together.

Take a small handful of the mince and roll it into a ball about the size of a walnut between the palms of your hands. Repeat with the rest of the mince.

In a medium stainless-steel saucepan or wok, heat the oil to 150°C (300°F) over a medium heat. This should take about 10 minutes, but you can use a kitchen thermometer for accuracy. Slowly add the fish balls to the oil and cook for about 10 minutes. They should be golden-brown.

Use a spider ladle or slotted spoon to remove the fish balls from the pan and lay them on a tray lined with paper towel to remove any excess oil. Serve warm with sambal tomat.

Makes 350 g (12½ oz)

— 2 unripe green mangoes,
  coarsely grated
— 1½ tablespoons coconut oil
  (for a recipe, see page 97)
— 4–5 red Anaheim or
  Colorado chillies (see
  page 274), seeded and
  finely sliced
— 8 tabasco chillies, seeded
  and finely sliced
— 5 lime leaves, finely sliced
— 1 teaspoon shrimp paste
— ½ teaspoon sea salt
— 2 tablespoons granulated
  palm sugar

'This is a real treasure from my island, Nusa Penida, which we only make when mangoes are in season between November and February. In my family, my bibi (aunt) is the sambal poh expert, and so this recipe is dedicated to her. She always uses mangga lembongan fruits, which are native to Nusa Penida. At their ripest, they are sweet with thin, edible skins. However, when they're young, they provide the perfect amount of tartness, which plays nicely against the sweetness of the palm sugar, the heat from the chillies and the zing of the lime leaf. We normally pair sambal poh with mackerel (which happens to be in season at the same time as mangoes), grilled over a wood fire on the sand, but it works well with any kind of grilled fish, such as Be panggang (page 192).'

— *Wayan*

SAMBAL POH

GREEN MANGO RELISH

Place the grated mango in a medium mixing bowl and set aside.

Heat the oil in a small saucepan over a medium heat for about 3 minutes.

Add the chillies, lime leaf and shrimp paste to the mixing bowl and pour the hot oil over the top. Toss the ingredients together by hand, squeezing them gently between your fingertips to allow the flavours to combine, but being careful not to bruise the mango too much. Wash your hands well afterwards to prevent chilli from getting into your eyes.

Add the salt and sugar, then taste and adjust the seasoning to your liking. There should be an equal balance of sweetness, saltiness, pungency from the shrimp paste and sourness from the mango. Spread generously over grilled fish or serve as a side.

Serves 2

- 100 g (3½ oz) banana leaves,
  cut into 20 × 22 cm
  (8 × 8¾ in) sheets
- toothpicks

- 1 teaspoon palm sugar,
  chopped
- 100 g (3½ oz/⅓ cup) Base
  kuning (page 55)
- 1 × 300 g (10½ oz) snapper
  fillet, cut in half
- 1 teaspoon sea salt
- 2 tablespoons coconut oil
  (for a recipe, see page 97)
- 2–3 red (Asian) shallots,
  sliced
- 6 garlic cloves, sliced
- 1 long red chilli (see
  page 274), seeded and sliced
- 2 salam leaves
- 1 small bilimbi (see page 277)
  or green tomato, finely sliced
- 2 sprigs carum (lemon basil,
  see page 274)
- steamed rice (for a recipe,
  see page 111), to serve
- stir-fried vegetables or urab
  (see page 132), to serve
- Sambal matah (page 76),
  to serve

'Pepes be pasih is insanely popular all across Bali, particularly in
the coastal areas where you can easily get your hands on fresh seafood.
For this recipe, I've chosen snapper because this is what we ate growing
up. My mother also made this recipe using albacore tuna and octopus,
which you should certainly try, too. It's one of my favourite ways of
cooking seafood, as the banana leaf holds all the moisture in, the charcoals
provide smokiness and the spices bring punch, heat and colour to the dish.'
— *Wayan*

PEPES BE PASIH

SPICED SNAPPER GRILLED IN BANANA LEAVES

Add the sugar and base kuning to a small mixing bowl and use your
hands to massage them together until completely combined.

Season the fish with the salt and add it to the base mixture. Transfer the
fish to the fridge to marinate for 30 minutes.

Heat the oil in a medium saucepan over a medium heat. Add the shallot
and garlic and sauté for 3–4 minutes, or until translucent, being careful
not to let anything stick or burn. Set aside to cool, then toss with the
chilli. Once cool enough to handle, massage the marinated fish with the
shallot mixture.

Preheat a charcoal grill or barbecue.

Prepare the banana leaves for wrapping (see page 27), then follow the
guide on page 188.

Grill the parcels over a medium heat for about 8 minutes on each side –
the banana leaf should get a little charred as the fish steams inside.

Carefully unwrap the parcel over a bowl to catch all the juices.
Place the meat on a plate, pour over the juices and serve with steamed rice,
a side of stir-fried vegetables or urab and sambal matah.

PEPES BE PASIH WRAPPING INSTRUCTIONS (PAGE 187)

Place a salam leaf in each parcel, lay the fish on top, then place a slice of bilimbi or green tomato and carum on top.

Fold one side of the banana leaf over the fish, going with the grain of the leaf.

Fold the other side of the leaf over in a letter fold.

Fold over both ends and fasten them with toothpicks or traditional bamboo sticks.

LEMPET WRAPPING INSTRUCTIONS (PAGE 190)

Place a salam leaf in each parcel and add a small handful of fish on top.

Fold one side of the banana leaf over the fish, going with the grain of the leaf.

Fold the other side of the leaf over in a letter fold.

Fasten both ends with toothpicks or traditional bamboo sticks.

Serves 5

- 1 m (3 ft 3 in) banana leaves (about 200 g/7 oz), cut into 18 × 20 cm (7 × 8 in) sheets
- toothpicks

- 500 g (1 lb 2 oz) mackerel fillet, diced
- 200 g (7 oz/¾ cup) Base kuning (page 55)
- 100 g (3½ oz) fresh mature coconut meat, finely grated
- 2½ tablespoons coconut oil (for a recipe, see page 97)
- 2–3 red (Asian) shallots, finely chopped
- 6 garlic cloves, finely chopped
- 6 tabasco chillies, finely chopped
- 1 tablespoon sea salt
- 1 teaspoon ground white pepper
- 2½ tablespoons palm sugar, finely chopped
- 5 salam leaves
- steamed rice (for a recipe, see page 111), to serve
- Sambal matah (page 76), to serve

'Lempet are best described as grilled minced fish cakes. On Nusa Penida, we make lempet out of low-value seafood, such as shark and sea eel, but I love them best during the fishing season when we can get our hands on skipjack and mackerel. They're soft, spicy and smoky from the grill, and the banana leaves hold in all the moisture, which concentrates the flavour of the spices. I've suggested mackerel here, but you can get away with using any kind of white fish as well. The beauty of the spices is that they do most of the hard work, adding flavour, colour and an unapologetically Balinese aroma.'

– Wayan

LEMPET

MINCED MACKEREL GRILLED IN BANANA LEAF

Preheat a wood fire, charcoal grill or barbecue.

Using a mortar and pestle, crush the fish until it forms a rough paste. Add the base kuning and coconut and continue to process for another 4 minutes, or until everything is combined. Transfer the mixture to a bowl and set aside.

Heat the oil in a medium saucepan over a medium heat. Add the shallots, garlic and chilli and sauté for 3–4 minutes, or until all the ingredients have wilted. Transfer to a bowl and set aside to cool.

Add the shallot mixture, salt, pepper and sugar to the fish and mix together, adjusting the seasoning if needed. Set aside.

Prepare the banana leaves for wrapping (see page 27), then follow the instructions on page 189.

Grill the parcel for about 5 minutes on each side. Serve with steamed rice and sambal matah.

Serves 2

- wire grill net (if cooking over a wood fire)

- 80 g (2¾ oz / ½ cup) Base kuning (page 55)
- 100 ml (3½ fl oz) coconut oil (for a recipe, see page 97)
- 1 teaspoon sugar
- 1 kg (2 lb 3 oz) red snapper or baby albacore, cleaned and butterflied or filleted
- steamed rice (for a recipe, see page 111), to serve
- Sambal matah (page 76), to serve
- 1 lime, cut into wedges, to serve

Almost every coastal village has its own take on grilled fish. Some marinate the fish in base, others grill it clean and serve it with sambal. There are different fish preferences, too. In Amed, it's usually mahi-mahi or tongkol, and up north it's mackerel. On Nusa Penida, it's normally the fish with the lowest market value, as the more precious stuff is reserved to be sold.

We've chosen snapper for this recipe, but you could use any kind of fatty fish. A wood fire or charcoal grill turns out the best results, but a barbeque will also work just fine.

If you're using a whole fish, serve it as is on a plate lined with banana leaf. Use your hands to separate the best pieces of meat from the bones, pinching it together with rice and sambal. And don't forget a good squeeze of lime.

BE PANGGANG
GRILLED SPICED SNAPPER

Preheat a wood fire, charcoal grill or barbecue for 10–15 minutes to a high heat.

Whisk the base kuning with half the oil and the sugar until well combined and smooth enough to brush over the fish.

Pat the fish dry with paper towel and place it on a tray. Lightly drizzle the remaining oil over both sides to prevent the fish from sticking to the wire net grill or barbecue, then season with salt and pepper.

Place the fish in the wire net (if cooking over a wood fire) and brush it with base kuning on both sides. Place the fish on the grill over a medium–high heat, skin-side down, and cook for 5 minutes, lightly brushing the top with more base as it cooks. Turn it over, brush with base again and cook for another 3 minutes, or until the fish is nicely charred and the flesh is soft and flaky with a yellow tinge from the caramelised spices. Serve with steamed rice, sambal matah and fresh lime.

Tip

We like to use wood or coconut husks for the fire.

Serves 4

- 2½ tablespoons coconut oil (for a recipe, see page 97)
- 2 red (Asian) shallots, sliced
- 3 garlic cloves, sliced
- 2 tabasco chillies, quartered
- 100 g (3½ oz / ⅓ cup) Base kuning (page 55)
- 1 cm (½ in) piece fresh galangal, finely sliced
- 1 lemongrass stem, crushed and knotted (see page 28)
- 700 ml (23½ fl oz) fish stock (for a recipe, see page 72)
- 2–3 salam leaves
- 3 lime leaves
- 1 × 300 g (10½ oz) snapper fillet
- ½ teaspoon sugar
- sea salt and ground white pepper, to taste

Most villages along the coastline have their own formula for kuah pindang — some cooks throw in young papaya, some like to add cucumber, some use the whole fish — bones, head and all — and others prefer to use boneless fillets. This very basic version uses snapper. It's clean, glassy and makes for excellent comfort eating. Pair with rice.

KUAH PINDANG

FISH BROTH

Heat the oil in a medium stockpot over a medium heat, and sauté the shallot, garlic and chilli for 3 minutes, or until fragrant. Add the base kuning, galangal and lemongrass, and sauté for a further 3 minutes.

Add the fish stock and bring to the boil over a high heat. Then add the salam and lime leaves, and let it simmer for about 5 minutes.

Add the fish and sugar and season with salt and pepper to taste. Simmer over a very low heat for about 1–1.5 hours, or until the fish is cooked through.

Serves 4

- 1 kg (2 lb 3 oz) fresh octopus
- 200 g (7 oz) sea salt, plus extra for seasoning
- 150 g (5½ oz) white onions, diced
- 10 garlic cloves, crushed (see page 28)
- 1 celery stalk, cut into 1 cm (½ in) slices
- 1 leek, sliced
- 2½ tablespoons coconut oil (for a recipe, see page 97)
- 150 g (5½ oz/½ cup) Suna cekuh (page 56)
- 3–4 lime leaves
- granulated palm sugar, to taste
- ground white pepper, to taste
- steamed rice (for a recipe, see page 111), to serve
- Nasi sela (page 115) or Nasi jagung (page 116), to serve

'Gurita (octopus) brings back so many memories of life on Nusa Penida. When I was a kid my father often took me hunting in the tide pools at night, when the water was low. We'd look for baby octopus, shrimp and the small fish that hide in-between the seaweed plots. When we did catch octopus, my mother would always stir-fry it with suna cekuh – our go-to spice paste for seafood. In this particular dish, which is inspired by my mother's cooking, I feel the sweetness of the octopus is really brought to life by the punch of the garlic and the aroma of the lesser galangal. It reminds me of being young and free.'

– Wayan

GURITA SUNA CEKUH

OCTOPUS WITH SUNA CEKUH SPICES

Separate the octopus head from the tentacles, then cut the tentacles into 3 sections (2 × 3 tentacles and 1 × 2 tentacles) – you can ask your fish monger to do this for you. Place the octopus in a large bowl.

Add the salt and use your hands to massage it into the octopus for 30–45 minutes to help tenderise the meat (see Tip).

Place the onion, garlic, celery and leek in a pot, add enough water to cover and bring to the boil over a medium heat.

Carefully drop the tentacles into the stockpot, turn the heat down to low and cook for 2 hours, or until the octopus is tender.

When cooked, strain, discarding the vegetables, and set the octopus aside until cool enough to handle, then cut the tentacles into 2½ cm (1 in) slices.

Heat a wok over a high heat, add the oil and sauté the tentacles for 3–4 minutes, or until they're crisp on the outside.

Add the suna cekuh paste and lime leaves and stir-fry for 3–4 minutes. Season to taste with salt, palm sugar and pepper, and serve with rice and a vegetable dish of your choice, such as nasi sele or nasi jagung.

Tip

The shortcut for this is to use a stand mixer with the paddle attachment on medium speed for about 15 minutes.

Serves 3

- 1 tube of green bamboo – approximately 50 cm (20 in) long, cleaned
- jalikan (wood-fired stove, optional)
- approx. 300 g (10½ oz) banana leaves, or other mildly flavoured edible leaves

- 500 g (1 lb 2 oz) mackerel fillet, cut into 1 cm (½ in) cubes
- 5 sprigs carum (lemon basil, see page 274)
- pinch of sea salt
- Nasi sela (page 115), to serve
- Urab don sela (page 135) or Urab kacang (page 134), to serve

SHALLOT–GINGER
MARINADE
- 80 g (2¾ oz / ⅓ cup) Base bawang jahe (page 58)
- 1 red (Asian) shallot, finely sliced
- 4 tabasco chillies, finely sliced (optional)
- 3–4 lime leaves, finely sliced
- ½ cm (¼ in) piece fresh ginger, finely sliced
- 1 teaspoon Uyah sere (page 71)
- 1 tablespoon palm sugar
- 100 ml (3½ fl oz) Santen (coconut milk, page 94)

Jero Mangku Dalem Suci Gede Yudiawan shared this recipe with us in his north Bali kitchen. It's extra special because it's cooked in bamboo – an old-school technique that leaves the fish beautifully smoky and swimming in juices and spices. Yudiawan is a real champion for the techniques and flavours of his hometown, and this recipe is true to the style of the north in that it's seafood-based and deeply aromatic. It also pairs well with Nasi sela gayot (page 182) and a good, fresh Sambal matah (page 76). To make this recipe, you'll need access to young bamboo, and you'll probably have to build a fire pit in your backyard – but it'll be worth every inch of the effort.

JERO YUDI'S IKAN BUNGBUNG

NORTHERN-STYLE MACKEREL COOKED IN BAMBOO

To make the marinade, combine all of the ingredients in a large mixing bowl and mix well using your hands.

Add the fish to the marinade and gently toss with your hands until it is nicely coated. Add the carum and salt and set aside to marinate for 15–45 minutes in the fridge.

Meanwhile, prepare your fire. Make it high enough to stand the bamboo vertically inside it. If you're using a jalikan, you can just prop the bamboo up against the inside of the stove.

Stuff the bamboo with the marinated fish and seal the ends with scrunched up banana leaves (or any other kind of mildly flavoured edible leaves).

Place the tube in the middle of the fire or jalikan in an upright position, making sure it's engulfed by the flames, and cook for 15–20 minutes.

Carefully remove the bamboo from the fire or jalikan and let it rest for about 10 minutes.

Open the tube at one end and shake the fish onto a serving plate with a lip to catch all the juices. Serve with nasi sela and urab sela or urab kacang.

Above: Freshly caught tongkol (mackerel).

Serves 3

- 1 kg (2 lb 3 oz) albacore
  fillets, cut into 7½ cm (3 in)
  pieces
- 100 ml (3½ fl oz) coconut oil
  (for a recipe, see page 97)
- 250 g (9 oz / 1 cup) Sambal
  tomat (page 84)
- 2½ tablespoons Santen
  (coconut milk, page 94)
  or water
- 1 tablespoon palm sugar,
  roughly chopped
- 1 teaspoon sea salt
- 1 teaspoon shrimp paste
  (optional)
- steamed rice (for a recipe,
  see page 111), to serve

'This is the ultimate weeknight dish – the kind that is familiar, yet slightly different in every paon. Most of Bali eats fish – whether that's freshwater lake fish up in the mountains, catfish and river fish in the lowlands, or the likes of snapper, tuna and mackerel down by the sea. Most of the time, fish gets the sambal tomat treatment, meaning it's fried until crispy then simmered in sambal until the juices have evaporated and you're left with a sweet, hot tomato-chilli reduction. When I was young, you couldn't take me away from my mother's pindang. Actually, this is probably true to this day. You can add coconut milk for a richer sauce, or use water instead if you prefer a lighter dish. The terasi (shrimp paste) is optional – I like it because it creates extra umami, but feel free to leave it out.'

– *Wayan*

PINDANG SAMBAL TOMAT
ALBACORE IN TOMATO SAMBAL

Place the fish on a tray lined with paper towel. Pat it dry with paper towel all over and set aside.

Heat the oil in a large saucepan over a high heat for around 5 minutes, or until it reaches smoke point, and fry the fish for 3–5 minutes on each side, or until nicely crisped all over. Remove the fish from the pan and set aside.

Using the same pan and oil, add the sambal tomat and sauté over a medium heat for 2–3 minutes.

Add the coconut milk or water, palm sugar, salt and shrimp paste, if using. Stir and continue to cook for 4–6 minutes, or until the sugar and shrimp paste have dissolved.

Add the fish back into the pan and stir well, adding a touch more water if it looks dry. Stew the fish in the sauce over a low heat for about 10 minutes, or until most of the water has evaporated. When it's ready, the sauce should be thick, sticky and sweet – almost like a chunky, spiced tomato paste. Serve hot with rice.

Serves 3

- 2 tablespoons coconut oil
  (for a recipe, see page 97)
- ½ red (Asian) shallot,
  finely sliced
- 2 garlic cloves, finely sliced
- 80 g (2¾ oz/⅓ cup) Base
  kuning (page 55)
- 2 tablespoons Base genep
  (page 50)
- 350 ml (12 fl oz) Santen
  (coconut milk, page 94)
- 200 ml (7 fl oz) chicken stock
  (for a recipe, see page 73)
- 6 salam leaves
- 1 lemongrass stem,
  white part only, crushed
  (see page 28)
- 100 g (3½ oz) chayote,
  peeled, seeds removed,
  quartered and cut into
  1–1½ cm (½ in) pieces
- 600 g (1 lb 5 oz) Bekakak
  ayam (page 248), bones
  included, cut into rough
  chunks
- 1 teaspoon sea salt
- pinch of ground white
  pepper
- Lontong (page 120), to serve

'My grandmother used to sell this soup at her market stand. It's rich and creamy from the coconut milk and can be made even more substantial with leftover grilled fish or chicken. It's a one-pot wonder that goes well with rice, rice cakes and any kind of urab.'
– *Wayan*

SEROSOP
COCONUT-CHICKEN SOUP

Heat the oil in a medium saucepan over a medium heat for about 3 minutes. Add the shallot and garlic and sauté for 3–4 minutes, or until fragrant.

Add the base kuning and base genep and sauté for a further 2 minutes, then add the coconut milk, chicken stock, salam leaf, lemongrass and chayote and simmer for 15 minutes, or until the chayote has started to soften.

Add the chicken and cook for a further 10 minutes. The soup should be slightly creamy with a dash of yellow from the spices.

Add the salt and pepper, stir, and adjust the seasoning to taste. Serve with sliced lontong rice cakes.

Serves 5

- ½ tablespoon coconut oil
  (for a recipe, see page 97)
- ½ red (Asian) shallot, finely
  chopped
- 2 garlic cloves, finely
  chopped
- 2 tabasco chillies, finely
  chopped
- 100 g (3½ oz/⅔ cup) ground
  corn kernels, soaked in cold
  water for 10 minutes then
  rinsed
- 1 litre (34 oz/4 cups) chicken
  or vegetable stock (for
  recipes, see pages 73 or 72)
- 7 salam leaves
- 50 g (1¾ oz/¼ cup) Base
  genep (page 50)
- 2 tablespoons Base kuning
  (page 55)
- 1 small sweet potato or
  cassava, peeled and cut into
  1 cm (½ in) cubes
- 40 g (1½ oz) dried red beans,
  soaked for at least 6 hours
- 1 sweetcorn, kernels sliced
- 1 teaspoon sea salt
- 1 teaspoon palm sugar
- ½ teaspoon ground white
  pepper
- 60 g (2 oz) green amaranth
  leaves (see page 273), stems
  removed
- 15 sprigs carum (lemon basil,
  see page 274)
- 1 tablespoon Fried shallots
  (page 75), to garnish
- Pindang sambal tomat
  (page 200), to serve
  (optional)
- Sambal mbe (page 78),
  to serve (optional)

'Ledok-ledok is another Nusa Penida speciality – another earthy star from the island where rice doesn't grow. It is a type of porridge made from sweetcorn and brightened with vegetables. It's creamy, hearty and tastes of spices and herbs. You'll need to soak the beans for at least six hours, so it's wise to start this recipe a day ahead.'

– *Wayan*

LEDOK-LEDOK

SWEETCORN PORRIDGE

Heat the oil in a small stockpot over a medium heat for 3 minutes. Add the shallot, garlic and chilli and sauté for 3–4 minutes. Add the ground corn and cook, stirring, for 2–3 minutes.

Add the kaldu ayam or sayur, salam leaves, base genep and base kuning and bring to the boil. Reduce the heat to low and simmer for 15 minutes.

Add the sweet potato, beans and corn kernels and simmer for 30 minutes, or until everything is cooked through and the corn kernels are al dente.

Add the salt, sugar, pepper, amaranth and carum. If the porridge feels too thick, add a dash more kaldu ayam or sayur to thin it out. Continue to cook over a low heat for 10 minutes, stirring occasionally, or until the amaranth is fully cooked – it should be soft but not mushy.

To serve, top the porridge with fried shallots and serve on its own or with pindang sambal tomat and sambal mbe on the side.

Serves 5

- 150 g (5½ oz) fresh green
  papaya (about ¼), seeds
  removed and quartered
  lengthways
- 25 g (1 oz/¼ cup) roasted
  coconut (see page 92),
  coarsely grated
- 3 tablespoons Base genep
  (page 50)
- 1 tablespoon Sambal mbe
  (page 78)
- ½ teaspoon palm sugar
- large pinch of Uyah sere
  (page 71)
- fresh lime, to serve
  (optional)

BRINE
- 100 g (3½ oz/¾ cup) sea salt
- 1 litre (34 fl oz/4 cups) water

'Growing up in a village on a dry island, fresh vegetables weren't always accessible, so quite often my mother would cook gedang (young papaya) instead. Gedang is such a comfort food for me. It's great because it has an incredible texture that works well both fresh and cooked, and a gentle flavour that works well with strong spices. My mother would toss it through salads or stir it into stews. This urab recipe brings the freshness of young papaya together with a good hit of coconut and fried shallots.'

– Wayan

URAB GEDANG

YOUNG PAPAYA SALAD

To make the brine, add the salt and water to a medium bowl and stir until the salt has dissolved.

Submerge the papaya in the brine and soak for 30 minutes–1 hour. This will drain the sap from the papaya and emphasise its natural flavour.

Bring a large steamer pot to the boil. Add the papaya to the steaming basket and steam for 10–15 minutes, or until the papaya is al dente. Set aside to cool.

Grate the papaya and set aside – we like to coarsely grate the papaya to add a bit of bite, but feel free to choose your favourite grate size for this recipe.

Combine the papaya and coconut in a large mixing bowl and toss together using your hands. Add the base genep, sambal mbe, palm sugar and uyah sere and toss again, using your hands to gently squeeze and massage the ingredients together. Be mindful not to bruise the papaya too much – you want to massage the spices into the fruit and extract some of the juices but without ending up with a bowl of mush.

Season with salt and pepper to taste.

SEAWEED

A STORY ABOUT YESTERDAY FOR TODAY

For my generation, a book that features Nusa Penida's culinary culture also needs to share a bit of knowledge about seaweed. You won't find recipes using seaweed in this chapter, though, because historically, we didn't farm seaweed as we didn't eat it. Instead, seaweed was a cash crop that we started planting on Nusa Penida during the 1980s to sell to Hong Kong via middlemen. Everything else we farmed, foraged or fished was for our food security, but the seaweed we grew for our livelihoods.

Seaweed was the vehicle that enabled my family, and many other families along the north coast of the island, to provide for ourselves. It was not grown on land that was inherited; it was a hodgepodge of free-for-all shallow sea plots that anybody could stake out for themselves if they were willing to do so. Seaweed was my family's primary source of income when I was growing up. The entire family could help generate income working in the sea plots, even young children, and for this reason it took centre stage as a family activity and provider.

According to my mom, the year that I was born was the same year seaweed was planted in Nusa Penida for the very first time. My physical existence and the pervasive presence of seaweed in my life as a child are so intertwined on a cellular and spiritual level that I once said to my wife, 'Without seaweed, I do not exist.'

One of my fondest memories is when I was twelve years old and I spent the entire summer between my 6th and 7th school year farming seaweed. I had just graduated from elementary school and had two months off before starting junior high school. My neighbour, Ibu Su, had hired me to help her with her seaweed plots in front of my family home. The work involved tying small baby seaweed plants onto plastic lines that are 5 metres (16 feet) long, then tying those plastic lines to wooden poles in the shallow sea plots just offshore. Ibu Su paid me per line of tied seaweed, so it paid to work fast and tie as many lines as I could. She also paid me to harvest her large seaweed plants every two weeks. That summer I asked Ibu Su to hold the money she owed me until the summer school break had ended. She did so, and by the end of the summer I had earned a whopping Rp 500,000 – which at that time was a lot of money for anybody, but for a 12-year-old it was an absolute windfall. The money was enough to pay my entrance fees for junior high school, the entire year's tuition, my uniform, shoes, books and monthly school fees. I was ecstatic. I knew my parents had borrowed money from my older married sister to pay for my school. I could not have been more proud the day I told my mother that she didn't need to borrow money and that I could pay for my school fees all on my own with the money I had earned farming seaweed.

It was around the time when the seaweed on Nusa Penida was replaced by tourism, snorkelling and speed boats that I left, too. I was not in Bali. I was living in the US cooking food in a Michelin-rated kitchen, food that could not have been further from the cuisine of my island home. Not to paint a picture of an existential crisis or anything, no, I loved my job; I loved the kitchen and the crew I was cooking with. However, what I will say is that I needed to be removed from Bali and Nusa Penida for several years to truly appreciate my childhood experiences and cuisine and return home.

Now, the global COVID-19 pandemic has caused many people to lose their jobs, and those relying on tourism-related incomes are once again turning to seaweed plantations for their livelihoods. The hodgepodge shallow sea plots are back on the island for the first time in several years. Quiet are the transport speed boats anchored just offshore in front of my childhood family home, boats that would, were it not for the pandemic, be busily shuttling a daily mass of tourists between Nusa Penida and mainland Bali. I was surprised at first how comforted I felt seeing the newly planted seaweed plots, but now I understand why: seaweed is a tangible essence of my community's resilience and perseverance. Seaweed has helped me pay for my education and has helped my parents feed nine children, and today it might help the communities in Nusa Penida to bounce back from the current economic crisis. Or, it might not be the seaweed that helps but rather the tenacity and grit of the seaweed farmers themselves that gets them through. My beloved Bali will bounce back after this pandemic, of this I am certain.

FROM
THE PASAR

–

FROM
THE PASAR

–

FROM
THE PASAR

–

FROM
THE PASAR

–

FROM
THE PASAR

–

FROM
THE PASAR

SWEETS,

SNACKS AND

SAVOURY

DISHES FROM

THE MARKETS

PASAR SENGGOL GIANYAR

DATES AT THE NIGHT MARKET

When I was eight years old, my family sent me to live with a priest's family in the seaside village of Keramas, which is about 30 minutes from Gianyar proper. In Gianyar city, there is a well-known pasar senggol (night market) in the centre of town, and my foster family liked to take us kids there on the weekends. I remember it being fun, loud and crowded, with people of all ages eating and shopping their way along the corridors of stalls. There were Indonesian delicacies of all descriptions here, many of which I'd never seen on Nusa Penida.

School-aged kids would be eating sweets, the teenagers were digging into the savoury stuff (babi guling, nasi ayam, sate ikan, tum, pepes be pasih) and solitary diners sat quietly at their favourite stalls staring contentedly into bowls of chicken noodle soup, bakso or beverages made colourful with syrups, jellies and fruits. Shards of crispy spit-roasted pig rubbed shoulders with piles of warm pandan-flavoured cakes and giant woks of nasi goreng that spat smoke and oil into the atmosphere.

Much of the food on offer was cooked live from brightly painted kaki lima carts, and I could watch the vendors prepare the dishes in front of me and was mesmerized. Up to that point in my life I had only watched my mother cooking alone, at home, in the pre-dawn mornings, or watched groups of village men prepare ceremonial dishes outside the temple walls. But this scene was different. Here at the market, I saw a diverse group of vendors, women and men both, all hurriedly working, cooking and plating for eager customers who were waiting with anticipation for the hot, fresh food that would be served. I saw the joy in everybody's faces, vendors and eaters alike, and it opened my eyes to another level of community happiness grown out of the sharing of food and cooking. I wanted more of that in my life, that joy which is shared, even among strangers. A seed was planted in me to learn to cook, that I myself might be a part of that happy food scene one day.

The night markets are different from the morning and afternoon markets in that they're less about produce and all about dishes. They kick off at 4 pm, continuing late into the night and feeding the masses as they head home from work or head out for an evening of revelling. I would say that the night markets are primarily enjoyed by the working class and the youth, as they are a place where everyone can try a lot of foods while not spending too much money. Also, a person knows what to expect – the same dishes are served each night, so it is a familiar, fun and inexpensive night out.

This is why I started to bring Mary, my wife, to Pasar Senggol Gianyar when we first started dating. It was also an opportunity to get out of Ubud, which, to me, was full of tourists and unfamiliar food. The night market was a safe space where we could get to know each other away from the scrutiny of family or co-workers. I also took a lot of pleasure in introducing Mary to my favourite childhood foods and treats. It was a way for me to express a bit of myself without having to directly say, 'this is me'. I think she appreciated being treated like a 'normal' girlfriend as well, which came as a challenge on Nusa Penida, where she was the only foreigner at the time, or likewise, in Ubud, where she was often mistaken for a tourist who was with her local guide (me!). We made Pasar Senggol Gianyar our go-to date night on payday at the end of every month.

When Mary and I started frequenting the market together, the scenes were pretty much the same as when I came as a child – busy, bright and loud. We had our dishes that we never strayed from, so we'd stall-hop, often starting with half-a-dozen skewers of spiced fish sate, followed by a serving of suckling pig or chicken betutu to share. The super simple grilled chicken dish known as ayam bakar was another favourite. The vendors glazed the birds with coconut oil and cooked them over fires built from coconut husks. It was sweet, earthy and smoky and reminded me of home. We'd always finish with sumping waluh, small rice and tapioca parcels stuffed with pumpkin (squash) and steamed in banana leaves, or a kind of dessert-cocktail known as es cendol made from shaved ice, coconut milk, pandan leaves, rice-flour jelly and palm sugar.

Nowadays, it seems the young generation is more likely to visit one of the shopping malls that have recently sprung up in Bali rather than a night market. The local food vendors have been replaced by fast food chains selling boba tea, mayo-drenched sushi, hamburgers and fried chicken. I guess times change everywhere, not only in Bali, but I think mall culture has put us in the position where our youth, at least youth living in urban areas with shopping centres, know more about cooking imported Western foods than they do Balinese cuisine. Some of our heritage is getting lost. Again, I hope I can have a positive influence in this regard. I have a lot of young Balinese cooks in my kitchens – sometimes they are straight out of high school or completing a school internship – and I'm teaching them how to cook local cuisine for what might be their very first time. This gives me hope. It's important to inspire the younger generations to learn about and relish the local cuisine, much like I learned to do by visiting the Pasar Senggol Gianyar as a young child. Food is an expression of where we come from. If we chefs can inspire young people to embrace their culinary heritage through joyful experiences, the payoff, I feel, will be priceless.

Serves 4

- 150 g (5½ oz / ½ cup) sea salt
- 150 g (5½ oz) green
  cannonball cabbage,
  quartered
- 150 g (5½ oz) snake beans
- 150 g (5½ oz) bean sprouts
- 300 g (10½ oz) Lontong
  (page 120), sliced into
  medium-sized discs
- 1½ tablespoons Kacang
  mentik goreng (page 108),
  to serve
- 1 tablespoon Fried shallots
  (page 75), to serve

PEANUT SAUCE
- 80 g (2¾ oz / ½ cup) Kacang
  tanah goreng (page 108)
- 3 garlic cloves
- 6 tabasco chillies, sliced
- 220 ml (7½ fl oz) warm water
- 1 tablespoon Fried shallots
  (page 75)
- 1½ tablespoon kecap manis
- 1 teaspoon lime juice
- 1 teaspoon sea salt

Tipat cantok is one of those dishes that tastes, looks and feels a little bit healthy and a little bit naughty all at once. When it's served at the markets, it's a joy to watch all the components being chopped, tossed and bundled together in brown paper – little parcels of peanut-fuelled nourishment to start the day. The key to any great tipat cantok is balance. You want it to be saucy, spicy, sweet and savoury. There should be a nice amount of crunch from the vegetables and starchiness from the rice cakes. Once you've mastered your perfect formula, you'll want it for breakfast, lunch and dinner.

TIPAT CANTOK
VEGETABLES AND RICE CAKES IN A SPICY PEANUT SAUCE

To make the peanut sauce, crush the kacang goreng, garlic and chilli into a paste using a mortar and pestle, gradually adding small amounts of warm water until the peanuts become creamy. Then add the fried shallots, kecap manis, lime juice and sea salt and continue crushing until everything is combined. When it's ready, the peanut sauce should be a light brown colour. Adjust the seasoning to taste and set aside.

In a large stockpot, add 3 litres (101 fl oz / 12 cups) water and the salt, and bring to the boil over a medium heat. Add the cabbage and snake beans and cook for about 10 minutes. Remove the vegetables from the pot using a slotted spoon and submerge them in a large bowl filled with ice water to stop them cooking.

Add the bean sprouts to the boiling water and cook for about 5 minutes. Remove from the pot using a slotted spoon and transfer to a large mixing bowl to cool.

Add the cabbage, snake beans and lontong to the bean sprouts, pour over the peanut sauce and toss, making sure everything is liberally coated in the sauce. Adjust the seasoning to taste by adding more salt, lime juice and kecap manis if needed.

Serve with kacang goreng and fried shallots sprinkled over the top.

SATE TUSUK

TWO SIMPLE SATES

Sate tusuk is the most straightforward kind of sate – just marinated meat on skewers. It's often made with chicken, pork or seafood, and it's deeply loved in all parts of Bali. One of our favourite pastimes together is sitting by a sate vendor in a cloud of smoke, waiting for the meat to cook over the coals. There are a few different marinades for sate tusuk. We've included two here: the sweet and spicy sate plecing from Singaraja in the island's north, and sate sere tabia, which is tangy and zingy from the tamarind and lime. Serve with steamed rice (see page 111) or Lontong (page 120).

Makes 50 skewers

- 1 kg (2 lb 3 oz) pork neck, diced into 2½ cm (1 in) cubes
- 50 thin bamboo skewers, soaked in water for 20 minutes

SATE PLECING MARINADE
- 300 g (10½ oz) Lombok chillies (see page 274), seeds removed and sliced
- 50 g (1¾ oz) tabasco chillies, finely sliced
- 4 red (Asian) shallots, roughly chopped
- 8 garlic cloves, roughly chopped
- 2 small roma (plum) tomatoes, seeds removed, sliced
- 100 ml (3½ fl oz) coconut oil (for a recipe, see page 97)
- 2 teaspoons sea salt
- 2 tablespoons palm sugar, chopped
- 1 teaspoon shrimp paste

SATE PLECING
SPICY PORK SATE FROM THE NORTH

Using a mortar and pestle, crush or blend the chillies, shallots, garlic and tomato into a fine paste.

Heat the coconut oil in a wok over a high heat for about 3 minutes and add the chilli paste. Cook for about 4 minutes, then reduce the heat to low and cook for a further 30 minutes, stirring every 10–15 minutes to make sure nothing sticks or burns.

Add the salt, sugar and shrimp paste and continue to simmer for 10–15 minutes, or until thick and fragrant. Take off the heat and transfer to a small mixing bowl. Fill a larger bowl with iced water and place the smaller bowl inside to allow the paste to cool completely.

Combine the pork with 250 g (9 oz) of the marinade (keep some aside to use as a sambal), giving it a good toss with your hands, cover and place in the fridge to marinate for at least 1 hour.

Preheat a charcoal grill or a barbecue.

Add four pieces of the pork onto each skewer and grill for about 3 minutes on each side, or until the meat is firm. Serve with rice or lontong and the rest of the marinade.

Makes 25 skewers

- 500 g (1 lb 2 oz) chicken breast, skin removed, cut into 2½ cm (1 in) cubes
- 25 thin bamboo skewers, soaked for 20 minutes

SATE SERE TABIA MARINADE
- 100 g (3½ oz) long red chillies (see page 274), seeds removed, sliced
- 8–10 tabasco chillies, finely sliced
- 1 teaspoon shrimp paste
- 2 teaspoons tamarind pulp or paste
- 1 teaspoon lime juice
- 2 tablespoons sea salt
- 3 teaspoons palm sugar

SATE TUSUK SERE TABIA
CHICKEN SATE WITH TAMARIND-CHILLI SAUCE

Using a mortar and pestle, crush the chillies into a smooth paste. Add the remaining marinade ingredients and crush to combine. Transfer to a bowl and set aside.

Place the chicken in a mixing bowl, add the marinade and toss it by hand until the chicken is nicely coated. Let it marinate in the fridge for 1 hour.

Preheat a charcoal grill or a barbecue.

Add four pieces of the chicken onto each skewer and grill for 3 minutes on each side, until the meat is cooked through, golden-brown on the outside and the marinade has started to caramelise. Serve with rice or lontong and sautéed greens.

Makes 10 cakes

- 500 g (1 lb 2 oz) banana
  leaves

- ¼ Japanese or butternut
  pumpkin (squash), peeled
  and coarsely grated
- 200 g (7 oz) rice flour
- 50 g (1¾ oz) mature coconut
  meat, finely grated
- 4 tablespoons Santen
  (coconut milk, page 94)
- 80 g (2¾ oz / ⅓ cup)
  granulated palm sugar
- 1 teaspoon sea salt
- 90 ml (3 fl oz) water

For both of us, no visit to the markets is complete without stopping at a jaja (traditional cake or sweets) seller. Their stalls are piled high with little individual cakes, made by hand in the earliest hours of the morning by the dadong (grandmothers) of the household.

Jaja are traditionally made from palm sugar, rice or rice flour and sometimes tapioca or ground cassava. They are dense, sticky, smoky and flavoured with local fruits or pandan leaves. The best kinds are cooked and wrapped in palm or banana leaves.

Rockstar jaja makers have cult followings and normally sell out long before the markets close. To get your fill, it's wise to have your alarm clock set for before dawn. However, in case you're not a morning person, you can always make your own. There are a few different takes on these soft, pillowy cakes; some have banana-filled centres and others are made sweet with chunks of golden jackfruit. We've chosen to highlight our combined favourite, sumping waluh, which are made from little flecks of grated pumpkin bound together by rice flour and coconut milk.

SUMPING WALUH

STEAMED PUMPKIN CAKES

Combine the pumpkin, rice flour, grated coconut, coconut milk, sugar and salt in a medium mixing bowl and mix together. The mixture will be sticky and crumbly. Pour the water in little by little to thicken the batter. Set aside until you're ready to wrap.

Fill a large steaming pot with water and bring to the boil. The water level should be 2½ cm (1 in) below the centre steam rack.

Prepare the banana leaves for wrapping (see page 27) and use the guide opposite to wrap the filling in the banana leaves.

Place the parcels in the steaming pot, cover and steam over a medium heat for about 30 minutes. When ready, remove them from the pot and place on a tray or plate to cool. Serve at room temperature with piping hot tea or coffee.

Add a large spoonful of the pumpkin mix to each parcel.

Fold one side over the filling, going with the veins of the leaves, not against them.

Fold over the other side, making sure the leaves overlap.

Fold in the ends to close the parcel. You won't need to fasten them to close.

Serves 5

— 700 ml (23½ fl oz) coconut
  oil (for a recipe, see page 97)
— 5 whole saba or ladyfinger
  bananas (see page 273),
  cut in half lengthways

BATTER
— 130 g (4½ oz) rice flour
— 1 tablespoon cornflour
  (cornstarch)
— 120 ml (4 fl oz) water
— 1 tablespoon Santen (coconut
  milk, page 94)
— 2 teaspoons granulated palm
  sugar
— 1 teaspoon sea salt

Nothing says Balinese breakfast better than a brown paper bag full of godoh. These sweet, crispy fried bananas are almost universally recognised, and for good reason. The batter is light and super crunchy, the bananas become soft and richly flavoured from the heat, and when they're made traditionally using good-quality coconut oil, those flavours sing through, too. You can serve them the fancy way with Gula Bali syrup (page 98) and a dusting of grated coconut, or you can dish them up as they are, plain and simple, with a cup of coffee.

GODOH

DEEP-FRIED BANANAS

For the batter, combine all of the ingredients in a large bowl and mix well.

In a medium frying pan or wok, heat the oil to 150°C (300°F) over a medium heat. This should take about 10 minutes, but you can use a kitchen thermometer for accuracy.

Add the banana to the batter and toss, making sure the banana pieces are completely and evenly coated.

Slowly drop the battered bananas into the oil, one at a time, and deep-fry them for 8–10 minutes, or until the fritters are golden-brown and float to the surface. Remove the fritters using tongs and place them on a tray lined with a paper towel to remove any excess oil. Eat when they're cool enough to handle but still nice and warm.

Serves 4

- 300 ml (10 fl oz) Santen
  (coconut milk, page 94)
- 400 ml (13½ fl oz) water
- 1 vanilla bean, split
  lengthways, seeds scraped
- 2 pandan leaves, knotted
  (see page 28) and squeezed,
  plus an extra leaf, to garnish
- 75 g (2¾ oz) rice flour
- 1 teaspoon sea salt
- Gula Bali (page 98), to serve

This is such an interesting, comforting, mind-blowingly simple dessert. The kind of thing pine for on a rainy day. Basically, it's a type of rice pudding made from rice flour instead of cooked rice, with santen (coconut milk) instead of dairy and with plenty of perfume from the pandan leaves.

Texturally it resembles custard – smooth, soft and creamy. There's a nice contrast between the sweetness and the saltiness, and when it's cooked over a wood fire you get the addition of smokiness, which is always a winner in our books.

BUBUR SUMSUM
PANDAN AND RICE PUDDING

In a medium saucepan, combine 150 ml (5 fl oz) of the coconut milk with 200 ml (7 fl oz) of the water. Add the vanilla bean (pod and seeds) and pandan leaves and slowly bring to the boil over a medium heat.

Meanwhile, combine the remaining coconut milk, the rice flour, salt and the remaining water in a medium mixing bowl and stir together until all the flour has been incorporated and there are no lumps.

Add the rice flour mixture to the boiling coconut milk, turn the heat down to medium and gently simmer for about 8 minutes, whisking continuously. When the pudding starts to thicken and is sticking to the whisk, reduce the heat to low and whisk continuously for 2 minutes. You'll know it's ready when it becomes super thick, like a paste or blended rice pudding, but without the chunks.

Remove the pan from the heat and take out the pandan leaves and vanilla pod. Pour the pudding into four separate ramekins or small bowls. Serve warm, with a generous drizzle of gula Bali and a sliver of pandan leaf on top.

Serves 4

— 1 large young coconut (you'll
   need about 1 litre/34 fl oz/
   4 cups coconut water)
— 240 g (8½ oz) ice cubes or
   crushed ice
— 2 tablespoons Gula Bali
   (page 98)
— 1 lime, sliced

This is the ultimate refresher. Es kuwud is an extra fun take on coconut water with gula Bali and lime. It's sold at markets, in warungs (local eateries) and by mobile street vendors, sometimes with additional slices of honeydew melon and selasih (basil seeds).

Here, we've shared a very classic version. You can use crushed ice and serve it in an ice-cream dish to make it work as a dessert. If you're serving it as a drink, grab a tall glass and use regular ice cubes – just make sure you have a spoon handy for scooping up the coconut meat as you sip and slurp away.

ES KUWUD

YOUNG COCONUT WATER WITH PALM
SUGAR SYRUP, LIME AND ICE

Open the top of the coconut with a cleaver (see page 92) and pour the coconut water into a large pitcher. Set aside.

Using a small spoon, carefully scrape the soft coconut flesh from the shell into a medium bowl in thin, long strips. Be mindful not to press the spoon too hard against the shell – you only want the young flesh on your spoon without any of the bitter shell lining. Set aside.

Evenly divide the ice, gula Bali and coconut meat between four tall drinking glasses and top each glass with coconut water. Finish with a squeeze of lime and serve immediately.

RARE AND
CEREMONIAL

–

RARE AND
CEREMONIAL

–

RARE AND
CEREMONIAL

–

RARE AND
CEREMONIAL

–

RARE AND
CEREMONIAL

–

RARE AND
CEREMONIAL

RITUAL FARE,

SPECIAL

OCCASION

DISHES

AND HEALING

FOODS

FOOD
AND THE
UNIVERSE

Cooking is just one of the many ways we connect with the universe. And when we speak about the universe, we're talking about the plants and the animals; water, earth, fire, air and ether; the stars and the planets; and all the divine energies that bring these things into being. Our spiritual belief system is a concoction of Hinduism (by way of traders and priests who came to Indonesia from India), Buddhism, Tantra and Bali's own animistic philosophies. We believe in a Supreme God and its many manifestations (see page 102), in karma, and in the atman (soul). And we worship in nature, underneath great trees, beside rocks and at the feet of mountains, by the edge of lakes, at freshwater springs, at the meeting of rivers, and, of course, by the ocean, because we believe the divine exists in all of these places. Our entire lives are synched to the natural world, even before we're physically reborn – and we say reborn because, like the Hindu followers of India, we live by the laws of reincarnation.

The way we acknowledge everything we see, hear, taste and feel as being part of the greater universe around and within us encourages us to pay close attention to everything around and within us. We understand that we're a slice of something much bigger – the cosmos – which we converse with through prayer, ritual, and, as we've explored in the pages of this book, food.

This dialogue starts on the farms and in the rice fields, where planting, harvesting and other seasonal rituals are bound to the cycles of the moon and sun. Then it trickles into the kitchen, where it zeroes in on the elements that help turn raw ingredients into edible dishes. In the thousands of temples and shrines across the island, food is presented to higher and lower forces alike, every single day. During larger ceremonies, hand-rolled dough monuments depicting Bhur, Bwah and Swah (the elemental, human and heavenly realms) pop against sacrificial grilled meats, ornate towers of pig's fat and entrails, and cylindrical arrangements of fruits and cakes laid out for the invisible beings to absorb. After all, only once all the residents of the universe are appeased, can we coexist in equilibrium.

Celebratory feasts and the dishes that come with them are laced with meaning. They are laboriously prepared, intricately spiced and sometimes colour-coded to pique our senses, appeal to certain energies and remind us that life is a multifaceted experience. Raw pork meat and blood might be tossed with coconut, shrimp paste, vegetables and spices in a symbolic act of creating balance. Rice is tinged yellow to represent the knowledge of the goddess Saraswati radiating from within, and is paired with a palate-activating shot of tamarind juice, sea salt and gula Bali to help us communicate her wisdom with clarity. Suckling pigs – spit-roasted until their skins are as glorious, golden and crisp as thick toffee – are made to represent gratitude and invite prosperity, among other blessings.

So, our food is a gift and a teacher – an energy source, an offering and a miracle from the earth. A perfect instrument, some might say, to express our love for our inner and outer home, the universe.

Following pages, from left: Offerings to the rice deity Dewi Sri; Wayan's auntie making jaja begina (a type of traditional cake); Saiban offerings ready to be distributed around the compound; Offerings for an odalan (festival) at Maya's home.

For both of us, betutu spells celebration, and we've both eaten it too many times to count. It's the star of almost every family feast, is used as an offering for specific rituals and is often served to priests in a tradition known as rayunan. This dish is usually reserved for special occasions, and it's easy to understand why. Traditionally, the whole bird (chicken or duck if it's for ceremonial purposes) is massaged and stuffed with base, wrapped tightly in banana leaves or the bottom end of a jambe palm (areca palm) branch and smoked overnight in a clay pot covered with burning rice husks. Some cooks dig a hole and cook it in the earth. Professional betutu specialists have bespoke wood-powered ovens to do the trick.

When the birds emerge from the smoke chamber, they're dark, fragrant and delicate. The meat almost drips off the bone. The combined powers of the various roots, herbs and leaves that go into the base create a deeply earthy flavour. The spice-tinged juices, held in by the leaf or bark wrapping, are served as a sauce alongside the main dish – more often than not spooned generously over steamed rice and vegetables.

Different parts of the island, of course, have their own riffs on the dish. In Gilimanuk, in west Bali, it's supercharged with chillies, and in the inner parts of the island, the focus is on subtlety and smoke.

This recipe is inspired by Ubud's style of betutu, which is normally cooked using the clay pot method. We've tweaked the process a little to save you from spending 10–12 hours on oven guard, but the flavours are just as rewarding. In case that you do have 12 hours, bags of rice husks, coconut husks and a large clay pot handy, we've included the traditional method as well.

For the best results, brine the bird for four hours before you marinate it, and when you're massaging the duck with the base, do it with gusto – until the bones crack – for extra tenderness and flavour.

- 2 banana leaves
  (60 × 60 cm/23½ × 23½ in)
- toothpicks

- 1 × 2 kg (4 lb 6 oz) duck,
  cleaned
- 100 g (3½ oz) fresh cassava
  leaves or kale
- 5 salam leaves
- sea salt, to taste
- 400 g (14 oz/1½ cup) Base
  genep (page 50)
- 3 lemongrass stems, crushed
  and knotted (see page 28)

BEBEK BETUTU
UBUD-STYLE SMOKED DUCK

Rinse the duck, pat it dry with paper towel and place it in the fridge until ready to use.

Bring a large saucepan of heavily salted water to the boil over a medium heat. Blanch the cassava or kale leaves for around 3–4 minutes, strain, then submerge in an ice bath to stop the cooking. Using your hands, squeeze the leaves to remove as much excess water as possible, then transfer them to a small bowl. Massage the leaves with salt to taste and about 4 tablespoons of the base genep and set aside.

Rub the whole duck with the remaining base, going all the way into the stomach and cavity of the bird. Stuff the seasoned cassava leaves, lemongrass and salam leaves into the cavity of the duck and close it with a toothpick or metal skewer. Let the duck marinate for about 4–5 hours in the fridge.

Preheat the oven to 160°C (320°F).

Prepare the banana leaves for wrapping (see page 27), and place the duck in the centre. Wrap the leaves around the duck and fasten them shut with toothpicks; ensure the parcel is well sealed. You want the duck to be wrapped tightly, like a gift in brown paper. Then, wrap the banana-leaf parcel in aluminium foil, place it on the middle rack in the oven and roast for about 3 hours.

Once it's cooked, carefully unwrap the parcel over a mixing bowl and pour the juices into a small jug or bowl to serve alongside the bird. Serve as the centrepiece of a special meal.

TRADITIONAL METHOD

Follow the steps to the wrapping stage above.

Place the wrapped duck on the ground in an outdoor space away from anything flammable and propped up on a couple of bricks, so that the heat distributes evenly inside the smoke chamber.

Cover the bird with a wide-mouthed clay pot and evenly cover the pot with the rice husks. It should look like a small hill.

Surround the bottom with coconut husks, light them on fire and blow the embers to help the fire spread. You can also place a lit coconut husk on top to make sure the whole thing catches fire.

The pile should burn away gently, smoking the duck from the outside in. Let it burn away slowly for around 10 hours, checking the fire regularly to make sure it's burning evenly. If you're tempted, you can check the duck at this point, using a bamboo rod or large wooden tongs to carefully lift the clay pot from the ground – it will be extremely hot to touch, so be careful. When you unwrap the bird, do it in a large mixing bowl so that you don't lose any of those precious juices inside the wrapping.

If the meat is still pink, cook it for another hour or so – you'll need to use your intuition. When it's ready, the juices will run clear, and it should be fork-tender and darkly tinged from the combination of all the leaves, roots and spices.

Before we dive into the preparation of lawar, it would be wise to discuss its spiritual importance. More than a dish for our enjoyment, it is a symbolic feast for the various manifestations of god (see page 102), prepared during large ceremonial events in a ritual known as mebat. In these ritual contexts, either five or nine kinds of lawar are offered to the deities that represent the cardinal expressions, elements and directions of the universe. The lawar dedicated to Brahma, god of the south, is coloured red with fresh animal blood. Wisnu, god of the north, whose colour is black, receives a lawar of dark don belimbing (starfruit tree leaves). Iswara, god of the east, is offered a lawar made white with coconut flesh, and Mahadewa, god of the west, gets a lawar tinged yellow with spices. At the heart of the offering, there are various kinds of sates and urutan sausages for the destroyer god, Siwa. The recipes for these sacred formulas are guarded and passed down by the men of the banjar (a community group within a village), who are graced with the task of preparing them. They sit together, butchering, peeling, chopping and mixing, perhaps enjoying a nip of arak (traditional palm wine) here and there, to create these multicoloured banquets for the divine, of which the leftovers, or the blessed lungsuran, can only be consumed after the ritual is complete.

These, of course, are the crown jewels of lawar – there are plenty of simpler takes on the dish that are much more casual in their composition. Everyday lawars can be made from kuwir (muscovy duck), the crunchy inner part of the coconut shell known as kelungah, young fern tips, bamboo shoots, snake beans and more.

The star ingredient of this vegetarian lawar is young jackfruit, which is made creamy with grated grilled coconut. It's important to use young jackfruit, as it's milder and firmer than the softer mature fruit, which is best enjoyed fresh or in desserts.

Lawar is all about harmony, so when you're combining the various components of the dish, aim for balance, variety and aesthetic appeal. Serve it on its own with rice and sambal, with sate and urutan, or as the centrepiece for a special occasion menu.

Serves 5

- 150 g (5½ oz/¾ cup) sea salt
- 350 g (12½ oz/about ¼)
  young jackfruit, roughly
  chopped
- 8 snake beans
- 60 g (2 oz/⅓ cup) coarsely
  grated roasted coconut
  (see page 92)
- 60 g (2 oz/¼ cup) Base
  rajang (page 53)
- 1 tablespoon Sambal goreng
  (page 75), plus extra, to serve
- 1 teaspoon palm sugar,
  roughly chopped
- 2 teaspoons Uyah sere
  (page 71, optional)
- ½ tablespoon Fried shallots
  (page 75)
- steamed rice (for a recipe,
  see page 111), to serve

LAWAR NANGKA

YOUNG JACKFRUIT AND BURNT COCONUT LAWAR

Fill a stockpot with 2 litres (68 fl oz/8 cups) water, add the salt and jackfruit, place over a medium heat and bring to the boil. Cook for 30–45 minutes until just cooked but still quite firm. Remove the jackfruit using a slotted spoon and set aside until cool enough to handle.

Using the same pot and water, add the beans and blanch for 5–8 minutes, or until just cooked. Watch that they don't become soggy. Strain the beans and place in an ice bath. Once they've cooled, strain again and set aside in a small bowl.

Roughly chop the jackfruit along the grain and place in a large mixing bowl. Top-and-tail the beans and slice into small pieces. Place in the same bowl as the jackfruit, but keep the ingredients separated for now.

Roughly chop the grated coconut and add it to the bowl with the jackfruit, still keeping everything in separate piles.

Add the base rajang to the bowl and toss everything together using your hands. One at a time, and tossing between each addition, add the sambal goreng, sugar and uyah sere, combining everything well and giving the ingredients a gentle squeeze to make sure they are evenly spiced. Taste or smell and adjust the seasoning to taste. Finish with the fried shallots for crunch and serve with steamed rice and extra sambal.

Serves 5

- 250 g (9 oz) pork belly, skin on
- 110 g (4 oz/½ cup) sea salt
- 200 g (7 oz/about ⅛) young jackfruit
- 100 g (3½ oz/½ cup) coarsely grated roasted coconut (see page 92)
- 90 g (3 oz/⅓ cup) Base rajang (page 53)
- 1 tablespoon Sambal goreng (page 75)
- 1 teaspoon Uyah sere (page 71)
- 1 lime leaf, finely sliced
- 1 teaspoon lime juice
- Sate lilit be caleng (page 250), to serve
- Balung (page 246), to serve
- steamed rice (for a recipe, see page 111), to serve

Pork lawar is undoubtedly one of Bali's most popular dishes, and it's the only lawar that has pretty much the same list of ingredients across the island, namely young jackfruit, coconut, base rajang and sambal goreng. There's a lovely textural play going on between the soft meat, chunks of jackfruit and shards of grilled coconut. To enjoy it ceremonial-style, serve it with sate lilit be caleng, balung and rice.

LAWAR BABI

PORK, JACKFRUIT AND COCONUT LAWAR

Place the pork belly in a medium stockpot with 1 litre (34 fl oz/4 cups) water and bring to the boil over a medium heat. Turn the heat down to low and simmer for about 2 hours, or until tender.

Remove the pork belly from the pot and transfer to a large plate or chopping board to cool slightly.

Place the pork skin-side down on a cutting board and carefully slice the skin away from the meat, making sure it stays in one piece. Then, slice the meat into thin strips and dice the strips into small cubes. Do the same with the pork skin and combine the two in a large mixing bowl. Set aside.

Add 1 litre (34 fl oz/4 cups) water and 100 g (3½ oz) of the salt and the jackfruit to a medium stockpot. Bring to the boil over a medium heat. Let it simmer for about 15 minutes, or until the jackfruit is tender but not mushy.

Remove the jackfruit from the pot, drain any excess water and let it cool on a plate until cool enough to handle.

Clean away any spongy parts of the jackfruit, slice into thin strips, then give it a rough chop. Set aside.

Combine the jackfruit and coconut with the pork in a large mixing bowl. Toss together well using your hands or a wooden spoon. Add the base rajang, sambal goreng, uyah sere, lime leaves and remaining salt. Mix everything together by hand, giving it a little squeeze to absorb the base. Finish with a squeeze of lime and serve.

Serves 4

- 150 g (5½ oz / ½ cup) sea salt
- 150 g (5½ oz) fiddlehead
  fern, young tips only, woody
  part of stems removed
- 10 snake beans
- 100 ml (3½ fl oz) coconut oil
  (for a recipe, see page 97)
- 80 g (2¾ oz / ⅓ cup) Base
  rajang (page 53)
- 1 teaspoon Uyah sere
  (page 71)
- 100 g (3½ oz) minced chicken
- 3–5 salam leaves
- 30 g (1 oz / ¼ cup) roasted
  coconut (see page 92)
- 1 tablespoon Sambal goreng
  (page 75)
- 1 lime leaf, finely sliced
- 1 teaspoon lime juice

This is a light, vibrant green lawar with chicken that's been chopped very finely, almost like a larb.

LAWAR KACANG

BEAN, FERN AND CHICKEN LAWAR

In a medium stockpot, combine 1.5 litres (51 fl oz / 6 cups) water and the salt and bring to the boil over a high heat. Blanch the fern tips in the boiling water for about 3 minutes, then quickly remove from the pot using a slotted spoon and submerge them in an ice bath. Leave the pot on the stove to blanch the beans. Remove the fern tips from the ice bath and gently squeeze them using your hands to drain any excess water. Set aside.

Blanch the snake beans in the boiling water for 5–8 minutes, or until just cooked. Watch that they don't become soggy. Strain the beans and submerge them in the ice bath. Strain again and set aside.

Chop the cooked fern tips into uniform pieces, no longer than the length of a fingernail. Repeat this process with the beans and set both greens aside.

Heat the coconut oil in a wok and sauté the base rajang and uyah sere over a medium heat for about 3–4 minutes. Add the chicken and salam leaves and cook, stirring, for 2–3 minutes.

Add 3 tablespoons water and a pinch of salt, and simmer over a low heat for 8–10 minutes. Remove from heat and set aside.

Roughly chop the roasted coconut and add it to a large mixing bowl with the fern tips, beans and chicken. Mix everything by hand, then add the sambal goreng, lime leaf and lime juice and mix it again. Season to taste and serve.

Left: Flowers and offerings for prayer.
Above: Offerings for full moon.

Serves 4

– 350 g (12½ oz) pork rib or
  rib tip, cut into 1 cm (½ in)
  cubes
– 80 g (2¾ oz / ⅓ cup) Base
  genep (page 50)
– 150 g (5½ oz) chayote
  (optional)
– 1 tablespoon coconut oil
  (for a recipe, see page 97)
– 1 red (Asian) shallot, finely
  sliced
– 3 garlic cloves, finely sliced
– 4 tabasco chillies, sliced in
  half lengthways
– 1 lemongrass stem, crushed
  and knotted (see page 28)
– 4 lime leaves
– 1 salam leaf
– 1.5 litres (51 fl oz / 6 cups)
  chicken stock (for a recipe,
  see page 73)
– 1 tablespoon Fried shallots
  (page 75)

'Every ceremony or celebration involves food, and when pork is part of the spread, it's usually the star offering. More often than not, the meatiest parts of the animal are reserved for rituals, while the balung is set aside for feasting. When I was still on Nusa Penida and cooking for the village, this soup was one of my favourite special occasion recipes.'

– *Wayan*

BALUNG

PORK STEW

Rub the pork with half of the base genep, making sure the meat is evenly coated. Leave in the fridge for about 1 hour to marinate.

Meanwhile, if using, cut the chayote into quarters, rinse and remove the seeds. Then dice into 2½ cm (1 in) cubes. Set aside.

Heat the oil in a medium stockpot over a medium heat, add the shallot, garlic and chilli and sauté for 2–3 minutes, or until fragrant. Add the rest of the base genep and continue sautéing for about 2 minutes.

Add the marinated pork, lemongrass, lime leaves and salam leaf and cook, stirring, for about 3 minutes.

Add the stock and bring to the boil over a high heat. Reduce the heat to low and simmer for about 1 hour, or until the meat is tender.

Add the chayote, if using, and continue simmering for 20 minutes, or until the chayote is cooked through.

Season with salt and pepper to taste, and serve with a good sprinkling of fried shallots.

Makes 280 g (10 oz)

- 30 g (1 oz/approx. 18 cm/ 7 in) fresh turmeric
- 2 tablespoons (approx. 20 g/ ¾ oz) freshly grated lesser galangal
- 8 garlic cloves
- 4–5 tabasco chillies
- 350 g (12½ oz) mature coconut meat, coarsely grated
- 2 tablespoons coconut oil (for a recipe, see page 97)
- 4 lime leaves
- 2 lemongrass stems, white part only, crushed (see page 28)
- 1 tablespoon sugar
- 1 teaspoon sea salt
- 3–4 tablespoons Kacang tanah goreng (page 108), to serve
- 3–4 tablespoons Kacang mentik goreng (page 108), to serve

This is the ultimate rice topper. Saur is sweet and crunchy – you might even call it flossy. In some households, it's served alongside a small amount of rice with a sliver of chicken in the daily offerings we call saiban. From a culinary perspective, it's a must-have condiment for any celebratory meal, usually served on a large sharing plate alongside deep-fried peanuts and kacang mentik goreng. The idea is to grab a handful of each and sprinkle it beside or over the top of your rice for texture and an extra kick of flavour.

SAUR KUNING
FRIED SPICED COCONUT

Using a mortar and pestle, crush the turmeric, lesser galangal, garlic and chilli into a fine paste. Set aside.

In a non-stick frying pan, dry-roast the grated coconut over a medium heat for about 10 minutes, stirring occasionally with a wooden spoon to get the moisture to evaporate. Set aside.

Heat the coconut oil in a medium frying pan over a medium heat and sauté the spice paste, lime leaves and lemongrass for 2–3 minutes, stirring constantly, or until fragrant. Add the coconut and stir to combine with the paste. Add the sugar and stir again.

Reduce the heat to low and continue cooking until the coconut is golden and dry to the touch. Season with the salt, or to taste.

Transfer the coconut to a baking tray lined with paper towel, distributing it evenly, to cool down and absorb any remaining moisture.

Store in a jar or airtight container in the fridge for up to 2 weeks. You can also combine it with crispy fried peanuts before storing. Serve with kacang goreng tanah and mentik or as a condiment, sprinkling it over everything.

Serves 4

- 1 × 1.2 kg (2 lb 10 oz) chicken, head removed, butterflied with the breast-side down
- 200 g (7 oz/¾ cup) sea salt
- 2 litres (68 fl oz/8 cups) water
- 3 lemongrass stems, crushed and knotted (see page 28)
- 6–7 salam leaves
- 6–7 garlic cloves
- 100 ml (3½ fl oz) coconut oil (for a recipe, see page 97)
- 150 g (5½ oz/¾ cup) Base kuning (page 55)
- steamed rice (for a recipe, see page 111), to serve
- Sambal matah (page 76), to serve

'Bekakak ayam is butterflied chicken basted in a turmeric marinade and grilled over coals or a wood fire. On Nusa Penida, we offer this dish once a year to Dewa Baruna, the sea god, with hand-shaped cones of freshly cooked rice. Across the main island, it's used in the ornate multi-tiered offerings known as gebogan, which are carried on the heads of the village women to important temple ceremonies. It's got a sweetness to it from the spices and is charred from the fire.'

– *Wayan*

BEKAKAK AYAM

GRILLED CHICKEN

Wash the bird and pat it dry using paper towel.

Dissolve the salt in the water and add the lemongrass, salam leaves and garlic. Submerge the chicken in the brine and let it rest in the fridge for 3–4 hours.

Remove the chicken from the brine and pat the meat dry once more. Set aside.

Combine the oil and base kuning in a medium mixing bowl, then use a pastry brush to coat the whole chicken with the marinade, brushing it under the skin for even more flavour – keep any unused marinade for basting during cooking.

Return the chicken to the fridge and let it marinate for 1 hour.

Meanwhile, prepare a fire or a charcoal grill. A wood fire is always our preference, but you could also use a barbecue.

If cooking over a wood fire or charcoals, lay the chicken on grill wires roughly 15 cm (6 in) above the hot coals. Grill each side of the bird for about 15 minutes, flipping it every 5 minutes or so and basting it with the marinade as you go, until the meat is equally cooked on both sides and golden-brown all over. Serve with steamed rice and sambal matah.

Serves 5

- 25 flat, wide bamboo
  skewers, soaked for
  20 minutes (see Tip)
- meat grinder (optional)

- 300 g (10½ oz) pork belly,
  skin off, roughly chopped
- 200 g (7 oz) pork shoulder,
  roughly chopped
- 100 g (3½ oz/½ cup) Base
  genep (page 50)
- 1 tablespoon Uyah sere
  (page 71)
- 2–3 tabasco or bird's eye
  chillies (see page 274),
  finely sliced
- 10 garlic cloves, sliced
- 4 red (Asian) shallots, sliced
- 1 lime leaf, sliced
- 1 teaspoon ground coriander
- 1 teaspoon whole white
  peppercorns, crushed using a
  mortar and pestle
- 150 ml (5 fl oz) Santen
  (coconut milk, page 94)
- 1 teaspoon sea salt
- 1 tablespoon palm sugar,
  finely chopped
- steamed rice (for a recipe,
  see page 111), to serve
- Sambal matah (page 76),
  to serve

Tip

If you can't find the flat, wide
Balinese sate skewers needed to
hold the meat to the skewer, use
25 lemongrass stems, white part
only, instead.

The word lilit means to twist, wrap or coil. This is a ceremonial style of sate that often appears in offerings or is brought to the house as an invitation to a wedding and other significant festival events. It can be made from pork, chicken, duck or fish. The meat is massaged with spices, twisted around flat bamboo skewers and grilled over coconut husks. Even though it's become popularised in warungs (local eateries), restaurants and cooking classes, it's still very much categorised as a celebratory food, as the process of making it is quite involved – first you have to mince the spices, then the meat and then combine all the ingredients into a paste that's sticky enough to press around the skewers (a task easier said than done). But the payoff is worth the effort – the lesser galangal, ginger and palm sugar caramelise over the charcoals and the meat becomes soft, sweet and full of flavour, kind of like a Balinese-accented kebab on a stick.

SATE LILIT BE CELENG

SPICED PORK SATE

Grind all the pork using a meat grinder on the smallest possible setting. Alternatively, chop it into a paste using a cleaver – you don't want any large chunks, so chop it well, sweeping the outside parts into the middle of the chopping board and working it until it becomes a smooth, consistent mince. Once you've got a fine mince, place in a large mixing bowl.

Add the remaining ingredients and mix by hand for about 5 minutes. Make sure all the ingredients are well combined, squeezing the mixture between your fingers to ensure there are no chunks of sugar, salt or spice. The mixture should feel smooth and slightly sticky. Set aside.

Preheat a charcoal grill or a barbecue.

Gently press a small handful of the meat mixture against the skewer, twisting the skewer as you press to make sure the meat is neatly and evenly distributed and adding more meat as you go. The meat should cover about one-third of the skewer and resemble a small kebab in shape. As you twist, use your fingers to keep everything in place and add more meat where it's needed. Repeat this process until all the meat is skewered.

Place the skewered meat on the grill or barbecue and cook for about 3 minutes on each side, or until caramelised and cooked through. Serve hot with steamed rice and sambal matah.

- 30 flat, wide bamboo
  skewers, soaked for
  20 minutes (see Tip)
- meat grinder (optional)

- 400 g (14 oz) chicken breast,
  skin off, roughly chopped
- 200 g (7 oz) chicken leg,
  skin off, roughly chopped
- 3 tablespoons coconut oil
  (for a recipe, see page 97)
- 3 red (Asian) shallots, finely
  sliced
- 7 garlic cloves, finely sliced
- 100 g (3½ oz / ½ cup) Base
  genep (page 50)
- 2 teaspoons Uyah sere
  (page 71)
- 2–3 tabasco chillies, finely
  sliced
- 3 lime leaves, finely sliced
- ¼ teaspoon ground coriander
- 120 ml (4 fl oz) Santen
  (coconut milk, page 94)
- ½ tablespoon sea salt
- 2 tablespoons palm sugar,
  finely chopped
- steamed rice (for a recipe,
  see page 111), to serve
- Sambal matah (page 76),
  to serve

Tip

If you can't find the flat, wide
Balinese sate skewers needed to
hold the meat to the skewer, use
30 lemongrass stems, white part
only, instead.

This recipe is very similar to Sate lilit be celeng (page 250), except it calls for chicken instead of pork. You could also use duck – just add a little more seasoning.

SATE LILIT AYAM

SPICED CHICKEN SATE

Grind all the chicken using a meat grinder on the smallest possible setting. Alternatively, chop it into a paste using a meat cleaver – you don't want any large chunks, so chop it well, sweeping the outside parts into the middle of the chopping board and working it until it becomes a smooth, consistent mince. Once you've got a fine mince, place in a large mixing bowl.

Heat the oil in a wok over a medium heat and sauté the shallot and garlic for 2 minutes, or until fragrant, being careful to not let them burn. Place in a bowl to cool and set aside.

Add the shallot, garlic and all the remaining ingredients to the minced chicken and mix by hand for about 5 minutes. Make sure all the ingredients are well combined, squeezing the mixture between your fingers to ensure there are no chunks of sugar, salt or spice. The mixture should feel smooth and slightly sticky. Adjust the seasoning as needed (see Tip, page 155) and set aside.

Preheat a charcoal grill or a barbecue.

Gently press a small handful of the meat mixture against the skewer, twisting the skewer as you press to make sure the meat is neatly and evenly distributed and adding more meat as you go. The meat should cover about one-third of the skewer and resemble a small kebab in shape. As you twist, use your fingers to keep everything in place and add more meat where it's needed. Repeat this process until all the meat is skewered.

Place the skewered meat on the grill or barbecue, and cook for about 3 minutes on each side, or until caramelised and cooked through.

Serve hot with steamed rice and sambal matah.

Serves 6

- 1.2 kg (2 lb 10 oz/6 cups) Nasi kuning (page 112)
- 3 Taluh mepindang (page 144), halved lengthways
- 30 g (1 oz/¼ cup) Kacang mentik goreng (page 108)
- 120 g (4½ oz/½ cup) Ayam sisit (page 152)
- 5 snake beans, cut into 5 cm (2 in) pieces
- 6 Sate lilit ayam (page 252)
- 150 g (5½ oz) Saur kuning (page 247)
- Sambal goreng (page 75), to serve

This is a yellow rice dish that's served during the preparation phase of temple ceremonies. Put simply, it's a combination of nasi kuning with small servings of meat, vegetables, sambal and other condiments to create a bright, complete meal. The idea is to get a taste of each element with every mouthful, which is where eating with your hands becomes very helpful. You can either serve it buffet-style and let each diner do their own plating, or portion everything onto plates lined with banana leaf for a bit of extra sparkle.

NASI YASA

YELLOW RICE WITH CHICKEN, SATE, BEANS AND CONDIMENTS

Using a 250 ml (8½ fl oz/1 cup) capacity ramekin or similar as a mould, shape six equal portions of the nasi kuning on individual plates or on a large platter, and arrange the remaining ingredients around the mounds of rice. If you're serving it family-style, plate each element individually for your guests to help themselves.

- meat grinder (optional)
  piping bag (see Tip)
- butcher's twine
- 1 metre (3 ft 3 in) sausage
  casing or clean pork
  intestines

- 600 g (1 lb 5 oz) pork neck,
  cut into rough chunks
- 400 g (14 oz) pork belly, cut
  into rough chunks
- 250 g (9 oz/1 cup) Base
  rajang (page 53)
- 2 teaspoons Uyah sere
  (page 71)
- 1 teaspoon ground coriander
- 1 teaspoon ground white
  pepper
- 3 lime leaves, finely sliced
- ½ tablespoon palm sugar,
  chopped
- 1 tablespoon sea salt
- Sambal matah (page 76),
  to serve
- Sambal goreng (page 75),
  to serve
- lawar (page 241–43), to serve

'These pork sausages are an important ceremonial food and every region has its own style. When I was living in Gianyar, for example, we'd ferment our urutan in the sun, which aged the meat and brought out a funky flavour similar to salami but spicier. This recipe doesn't call for fermentation, but it is delicious and smoky with a nice amount of spice. This sausage can either be cooked fresh or smoked first. Smoked urutan goes a long way and can be kept in the fridge or freezer for up to 3 months. Plus, it has an added layer of depth from the wood fire. Here is the recipe along with three different cooking methods.'

– *Wayan*

URUTAN

GIANYAR-STYLE PORK SAUSAGE

Grind the pork using a meat grinder on a medium setting. Alternatively, chop it using a cleaver – you don't want any large chunks, so chop it well, sweeping the outside parts into the middle of the chopping board and working it until it becomes a consistent mince.

Add the base rajang and uyah sere and continue to mix by hand until everything is evenly combined. Add all the remaining ingredients and mix again until everything is combined.

Transfer the mince to a piping bag and add a fitting that's big enough for the meat to pass easily into the sausage casing.

Tie a knot on one end of the casing, or close it using butcher's twine, and place the tip of the piping bag in the open end. Slowly and gently squeeze the minced meat into the casing to create one long sausage, being careful to let as little air as possible in. Tighten the casing by squeezing the meat down until there's absolutely no air inside, and tie a knot at the end of the sausage, or use butcher's twine. Store the sausage, covered, in the fridge overnight.

Cook the urutan using one of the methods opposite and serve it hot with sambal matah or sambal goreng and your choice of lawar.

Tip

We prefer to stuff this sausage the traditional way, but if you've got the equipment, you can also use a sausage stuffing attachment for your meat grinder or food processor to stuff the sausage.

SMOKING

Preheat a smoker to 115–120°C (240–250°F). Place the urutan on the rack and smoke it for about 2–3 hours. When it's ready, it should be crisp on the outside and moist on the inside.

GRILLING

Preheat a barbecue or a charcoal grill to a medium heat. Roll the urutan into a coil and place it on the barbecue, or, if using a grill, place it on a rack about 10 cm (4 in) above the coals. Grill for about 15–20 minutes, flipping it every 5 minutes, until each side is golden-brown and just slightly charred.

BAKING

Preheat the oven to 170°C (340°F) and place the urutan in a coil directly on the middle rack with a baking tray underneath to catch the drippings. Bake for 30 minutes, flipping the sausage after 15 minutes.

On the Sunday after the Balinese-Hindu festival of wisdom, Hari Saraswati, worshippers flood the beaches, rivers, springs and water temples of the island to partake in a ritual known as Banyu Pinaruh. The day before, we ask for the blessings of Saraswati, the goddess of knowledge, learning and the arts, and offerings are laid, books are blessed and prayers are sent from the temples of schools, homes and other dedicated shrines. Then, on the morning of Banyu Pinaruh, a mass purification takes place. Spiritual bathers take to the island's waterways to activate Saraswati's magic through a practice known as melukat. We wash in nature and then again at home with a flower-scented water called yeh kumkuman. And then we feast. The traditional Banyu Pinaruh meal is a combination of yellow rice, kacang saur, slivers of fried egg and sliced cucumber, known collectively as nasi bira. These, of course, are just the core elements of the dish; it can be livened up with anything from smoked duck or chicken to spiced fried eggs or warm urab vegetables. But it's the rice with its bright turmeric tinge that carries the most meaning. It symbolises the knowledge bestowed by Saraswati radiating from inside us. The accompanying loloh tonic, made from tamarind and pressed sembung (ngai camphor leaves), is the internal part of the cleansing ritual. It's taken as a shot to titillate the tongue and awaken the Sad Rasa (six fundamental tastes of the universe). Sembung leaves are also highly medicinal, prized for their antibacterial and antioxidant properties, so as well as washing negative energy away from the tongue, loloh also provides its drinkers with a gentle detox. A cellular and spiritual deep cleanse, if you like.

Serves 5

- 1 red (Asian) shallot, sliced
- 1 kg (2 lb 3 oz/4 cups) Nasi kuning (page 112)
- 100 g (3½ oz/½ cup) Base genep (page 50)
- ½ tablespoon sea salt
- 1 teaspoon ground white pepper
- 2 tablespoons coconut oil (for a recipe, see page 97)
- 1 egg

TO SERVE
- 200 g (7 oz/¾ cup) Ayam sisit (page 152)
- 5 Sate lilit ayam (page 252)
- 50 g (1¾ oz/¼ cup) Saur kuning (page 247)
- 1 small continental cucumber, peeled and sliced
- 2–3 round green eggplants (aubergines), sliced
- 50 g (1¾ oz/¼ cup) Sambal goreng (page 75)
- 1 torch ginger flower (see page 277), finely sliced
- 50 g (1¾ oz) sprouted mung beans

NASI BIRA
CEREMONIAL YELLOW RICE DISH

Sauté the shallot in a medium frying pan over a high heat until crisp and golden. Remove the shallot from the pan with a spider ladle or slotted spoon and set aside on a plate lined with paper towel to soak up any excess oil.

In a large bowl, combine the warm nasi kuning and base genep, mixing it together with a wooden spoon until evenly combined. Add the shallot, salt and white pepper. Stir once more and adjust the seasoning to taste. The rice should be earthy and fragrant with a touch of spice. Set aside.

Using a non-stick pan, heat the oil over a medium heat for about 3 minutes.

Meanwhile, crack the egg into a small bowl, add a pinch of salt and whisk together.

Slowly pour the egg mixture into the pan and cook for about 3 minutes, then flip it over and cook for a further 2 minutes. Remove the omelette from the pan and lay it on a tray lined with a paper towel to cool, then fold the omelette in half and cut it into 5 equal portions. Set aside.

Using a 250 ml (8½ fl oz/1 cup) capacity ramekin or similar as a mould, shape five equal portions of the seasoned rice and place each on a plate surrounded by the ayam sisit, sate lilit, omelette, saur kuning, cucumber, eggplant and sambal goreng. Top the rice with the torch ginger flower and mung beans. Consume mindfully.

LUNGSURAN

BLESSED FOOD

My family and I are driving along the Kintamani caldera towards Ubud, having completed a tilem (dark moon) pilgrimage – five temples in eight hours, starting at the sea then moving north towards the mountains. Driving along this road late at night catapults you into a rather unexpected realm. Thick fog engulfs the road, swallowing up the houses, restaurants and souvenir shops that line the ancient crater. Along some parts of the drive, she-oaks pierce through the fog – tall and mysterious, just visible through the blue-white haze. When the crisp wind blows, it howls, spraying bursts of icy water across the windscreen. You could be forgiven for thinking you were in Scotland.

Pura Ulun Danu Batur, one of the six cardinal temples of Bali, was the final stop of our journey. It's perched above the holy lake Batur that nourishes the villages, rice fields and farms of the island's east. Weary but buzzing from half a day of devotion, fuelled by prayer and sweet, sludgy cups of coffee, we realise we haven't eaten dinner. 'Nothing will be open between here and Ubud,' my father says. 'Pass the lungsuran around.'

Lungsuran is offering food. During temple festivals or private pilgrimages, colourful woven baskets are packed with fruits and cakes, usually various types of jaja (traditional cakes or sweets), woven palm leaf offerings, flowers and a modest amount of sesari (money), which is collected by the officiating priests. These baskets are laid before the temple deities, so that the sari (essence) of the offerings might be absorbed by the universe – a symbolic feast for the cosmos. When the priests set down their bells, and holy water has been adequately sprinkled and sipped across the temple courtyard, the crowd rises to collect their offerings. The food component is now blessed lungsuran and the leftovers are fair game – free to be enjoyed by the worshippers themselves.

I reach into our keben (offering basket) and feel around for some recognisable form of nourishment in the darkness of the moving car. I score a salak (snake fruit), peel back its scaly skin and take in its crunch and sweetness. The children go straight for the jaja sirat – soft, stringy pancakes of gula Bali and rice flour, perfect for wrapping around sweet green bananas. My father snaps off a piece of jaja begina, which is a fried cracker of sorts, made from puffed rice and palm sugar. I secure the other half, pair it with a tart Kintamani orange and the end of a Beng-Beng chocolate bar that somehow made it into the mix.

Approaching Ubud, we roll down the windows and take in the warmer, humid air. We're ready for bed and the rows of closed restaurants don't faze us – we've already been fed by way of the gods.

Top: Offerings of fruits, woven palm leaves and flowers presented to a guardian spirit at the foot of a great tree.
Bottom: Baskets of offerings presented to the gods before prayer.

*Top left: Holy water being offered
to worshippers by a mangku (priest)
at the close of prayers.
Right: Baskets of food and offerings
being prepared before prayer.*

Serves 4

- 500 g (1 lb 2 oz) white sticky rice
- ½ teaspoon sea salt
- 350 ml (12 fl oz) Gula Bali (page 98)
- 1 pandan leaf, sliced, to garnish

'Jaje wajik are types of sticky rice desserts infused with pandan leaves and sweetened with palm sugar. It is a comfort snack for many Indonesians, and you'll find it across many of the islands. When I was a kid, my mother would always make this cake for festival days such as Galungan and Kuningan, or for Nyepi, our annual day of silence. The first batch would go into our offerings, but the leftovers were fair game. I always looked forward to my slice. Here is my mother's recipe.'
– *Wayan*

JAJE WAJIK
STICKY RICE CAKES

Wash the rice under running water until the water runs clear. Soak it in cool water for about 10 minutes, then strain.

Fill a steaming pot with water to about 2.5 cm (1 in) below the centre steam rack. Steam the rice for 10 minutes, then transfer to a large mixing bowl and soak it in 500 ml (17 fl oz/2 cups) hot water for 10–12 minutes, or until the water has been completely absorbed by the rice.

Return the rice to the steamer and cook for 10 minutes – it should be sticky at this point.

In a large saucepan, combine the rice, salt and gula Bali, giving it a good stir. Simmer over a very low heat, stirring continuously, until the rice turns golden – watch that it doesn't stick or burn.

Pour the rice into a 23 × 33 cm (9 × 13 in) non-stick baking tray, and gently press it down evenly with a spatula. Cover with baking paper and let the rice cool to room temperature.

Cut the rice into squares or rectangles. To finish, add a slice of pandan leaf on top for extra flavour.

Makes 400 ml (13½ fl oz)

SPICE EXTRACTS
- 8 cm (3¼ in) piece fresh young ginger, sliced
- 85 g (3 oz) fresh turmeric, sliced
- 50 g (1¾ oz) lesser galangal, sliced
- 1.35 litres (46 fl oz) filtered water
- 2 large lemongrass stems, white part only, finely sliced
- 2–3 pandan leaves, sliced
- 1 cinnamon stick
- 1 teaspoon cloves

LOLOH
- 50 ml (1¾ fl oz) ginger extract
- 75 ml (2½ fl oz) turmeric extract
- 50 ml (1¾ fl oz) lesser galangal extract
- 75 ml (2½ fl oz) lemongrass extract
- 50 ml (1¾ fl oz) pandan extract
- ½ tablespoon cinnamon extract
- 1 tablespoon clove extract
- 50 ml (1¾ fl oz) Gula Bali (page 98)
- 1 tablespoon lime juice

We often hear about jamu, the herbal beverages of Java that are well known for their healing properties. Bali's own plant-based potions, known as loloh, are equally as fascinating – and just as powerful. Loloh tonics are hand-pressed out of leaves, roots and bulbs. Some are sweet and herbaceous, some are bitter and green, and some are vibrant and lightly spiced. Many of them, in fact, are similar to jamu in essence. This loloh kunyit is made from pure ginger, turmeric, lesser galangal, lemongrass, pandan leaves, cinnamon and clove extracts simmered into a potent anti-inflammatory, immune-boosting tonic. You'll need to make the extracts from scratch, using whole ingredients. When it comes to loloh, powdered spices won't work, so if you can't find fresh lesser galangal, hunt around for the frozen stuff instead.

LOLOH KUNYIT
MEDICINAL TURMERIC TONIC

Dry-roast the ginger in a small frying pan over a medium heat for 5 minutes and set aside. Repeat this process with the turmeric and then the lesser galangal.

Using a food processor, blend the ginger with 200 ml (7 fl oz) filtered water and strain the liquid into a bowl, discarding the solids. Set aside. Repeat this process with the turmeric and lesser galangal.

Add the lemongrass and 350 ml (12 fl oz) filtered water to a small saucepan and bring to the boil over a medium heat, then reduce the heat to low and simmer for about 10–15 minutes. Strain into a medium bowl, discarding the solids. Set aside.

Add the pandan leaves and 100 ml (3½ fl oz) filtered water to a saucepan and bring to the boil over a medium heat, then reduce the heat to low and simmer for about 10–15 minutes. Strain into a bowl or jar, discarding the solids. Set aside.

Add the cinnamon sticks and 200 ml (7 fl oz) filtered water to a saucepan and bring to the boil over a medium heat, then reduce the heat to low and simmer for about 10–15 minutes. Strain into a bowl or jar, discarding the solids. Set aside.

Add the cloves and 4 tablespoons water to a saucepan and bring to the boil over a medium heat, then reduce the heat to low and simmer for about 10–15 minutes. Strain into a bowl or jar, discarding the solids. Set aside.

To make the loloh, combine all of the ingredients except the lime juice in a medium stainless steel saucepan and simmer over a low heat for 30 minutes.

Strain the liquid through a fine-mesh sieve into a pitcher. Place the pitcher in a large bowl filled with ice water for about 20 minutes to cool down the liquid.

To serve, combine 100 ml (3½ fl oz) of the loloh with a teaspoon of lime juice in a small glass.

Store loloh in a glass bottle in the fridge for up to 3 days.

Serves 5

- 100 g (3½ oz) daluman leaves (see page 128)
- 800 ml (27 fl oz) filtered water
- Santen (coconut milk, page 94), to serve
- Gula Bali (page 98), to serve
- ice cubes, to serve

'Originally, there was no recipe for daluman in this chapter, but it would be wrong to not talk about it in a book about Balinese cooking. Put simply, it's a kind of jelly made from two ingredients: daluman leaves and water. The smooth green leaves, shaped almost like a small elongated Bodhi leaf, are hand-squeezed, strained and left to set into a soft, chlorophyll-tinged jelly that's fresh on the palate. On Bali, they grow wildly by rivers, in forests and tangled among the grasses and shrubberies of private gardens, which makes finding them quite the adventure. Like many traditional Balinese plants, they come to you when nature provides them and rarely ever on demand. The first time I made daluman, my niang (grandmother) said, "Have this often, there's a lot of heat running inside you." She was right, for it's well known that daluman is an extremely cooling plant. On its own, daluman jelly is grassy and medicinal – the perfect antidote to the humidity of the equatorial climate. You could compare it to a cincau jelly, only without the sugar or any additional starches. Most of the time, it's served in an iced drink of fresh coconut milk and a palm sugar syrup called es daluman, which is sold at traditional markets, in some warungs (local eateries) and by mobile vendors on the side of the road. This is one of those rare super pure desserts from the past and a brilliant reminder of Balinese culinary sophistication at its simplest. So, in the case that you do come across daluman leaves on the island (or by some miracle anywhere else in the world), here's how to work them into jelly.'

– Maya

DALUMAN
COOLING LEAF JELLY

Rinse the daluman leaves well in a strainer under running water. Make sure they have made no contact with salt, as this will prevent the jelly from setting.

Place the leaves and water in a large mixing bowl and squeeze them liberally (you almost want to wring them), using both hands, for about 6 minutes, or until all the juices have been extracted from the leaves. When ready, the water will be dark green, bubbly and slightly sticky from the saps.

Strain the liquid into another bowl, discarding the leaves, and leave to set for about 30 minutes, or until it gives a little jiggle when tapped with a spoon.

Scoop a couple of tablespoons into a glass with a handful of ice cubes, top with coconut milk and finish with a swirl of gula Bali. Serve immediately.

FROM MAYA

This book is the result of great synergy between many hearts, minds and hands. It is also the legacy of a long line of ancestors, who I believe are the true heroes of Balinese cooking – they birthed it, shaped it and embodied it in ways that I can only imagine and wish to master in the years to come. And so, I'll close by firstly sending my gratitude to the cooks of this island's past who founded and passed down the knowledge in and beyond these pages from one generation to the next.

And then, we have the current upholders of the cuisine. All the women and men still with us today who devote a large part of their modern lives to traditional cooking – the foremost, for me, being my niang (grandmother). As I reflected on the journey of this book and how it came into being, I began to fully realise the scale of the divide between my niang's life experience and mine. *Paon* began as a mission to honour a food culture, but it quickly transformed into a study of an incredible way of life – beyond cooking and eating into full-bodied devotion. An entire existence shaped around the cycles of the earth, the laws of the sky and the power of the human heart.

Niang never experienced the thrills of being young and reckless; she's never known material abundance or a thriving career. She doesn't indulge in travel, leisure or personal passions. She claims to have never been in love. To many, her journey might be perceived as one of suppression, and yet her complexion is etched with lines that tell of a lifetime of laughter, and her heart, she tells me, is devoted towards the gods in the hope that they will love us back. She has lived a life of service for the greater good of others, and I'm humbled to have been part of this.

Bali is an island of many expressions. It can be both ancient and modern, light and dark, gentle and formidable. Our culture is at once open and fiercely protected. The landscape transforms and surprises in a matter of hours – in some cases minutes – and the flavours do the same. When so much is happening in the space of a considerably small island, there is a risk of character being lost to one particular power or another. However, our emphasis on tolerance and harmony ensures that many worlds, many faiths and many states of being are able to coexist on our land, which makes me confident that the regional cuisines of Bali have a bright future.

Our traditional ingredients, recipes and cooking methods could have died out many years ago. The jalikan (wood-fired stove) could have become extinct, the dangdang (clay rice cooker) could have been reduced to a museum display, and every spice paste could have been churned through a blender instead of a batu base (mortar and pestle). In some cases, these things are true. But because of the power of adat (tradition), as well as faith in god and in nature, Balinese food has persevered in a powerful way. It has transcended the lures of globalism and convenience, and its role remains deeply rooted in our cultural identity – it is my hope that this will remain true in the years to come.

FROM WAYAN

Food is a language full of heritage and stories. By writing this comprehensive cookbook on Balinese cuisine, Maya and I took on the phenomenal task of sharing our culture, geography, belief system, social structure, arts and more through the stories and language of our food. We are communicating who we are as individuals and who we are as a community of four-plus million Balinese people. The very act of cooking and sharing food is an act of self-expression and identity, and in this sense, food is the language we use to translate who we are to the outside world, as well as to ourselves. It is an honour and a privilege for me to have collaborated on such an important project – an honest behind-the-curtain look at Balinese food tradition and cultural identity.

I was quite shy as a kid, but these days I find joy and easy communication through cooking. I hope the readers and cooks who find their way to this book also find joy between the pages and in the recipes, and discover new ways to cook and eat. Not many people know this, but I have been speaking English for just ten years. My motivation to learn English increased tenfold after I was married to my American wife and decided I wanted to go to culinary school in the US. I wanted to gain the skills and knowledge needed to share authentic Balinese cuisine with the rest of the world. My mother tongue is a Nusa Penida dialect spoken by roughly 35,000 people. If you had told me twenty years ago that I would be travelling around the world cooking Balinese cuisine professionally and writing an English-language cookbook, I would have laughed – the idea would have been outrageous!

If I may, I'd like to take a moment to acknowledge the rarity that is this book – a collection of personal, authentic, unfiltered recipes and stories from Bali, told and written by Balinese, in English, for a global audience. When it comes to Balinese cuisine, many chefs and writers have been inspired by Balinese flavours, techniques and traditions through the years and have written about our food to some success, but how many times has a foreign cook gotten the flavours wrong? Or how many times have I picked up a book that proclaims to feature 'the food of Bali' but instead features foreign chefs who work in Bali? It is disheartening that this is how Balinese food is being represented when we Balinese are trying to keep our food culture alive and thriving – let's not forget that the true masters of our food heritage are the grandmothers, mothers, domestic cooks and priests in our lives, the vast majority of whom do not speak any English. Without the language literacy to share their knowledge, many of them are relegated to play characters in somebody else's story about Bali rather than representing themselves. Hardie Grant is a publisher that recognised the importance of inviting Balinese food professionals to represent ourselves, and I am very grateful for that. Maya and I have strived for authenticity of flavours, ingredients, traditional methods, equipment and regional recipes. As members of this thriving, vibrant, complicated Balinese culture and community, we have used our language skills and community network to access the hard-to-reach elders and villagers who are the masters of our cuisine in order to share their stories with the world. In effect, we are the translators of the food knowledge that our elders and ancestors have passed down through oral tradition.

I believe the key to preserving our Balinese food culture and knowledge lies in the education and professionalisation of Balinese youth, especially girls. Our elders hold the keys to our paons and our food rituals, and to share their knowledge we need to be able to read, write and cook. Just as language literacy and learning English was my ticket to a professional career in food, it can do the same for young Balinese women if we make the effort. Historically, women have often been overlooked for opportunities in education and professional careers, and it's time to change that dynamic by hiring girls – and to train them and support their advancement and independence – instead of sacrificing our daughters' education to support our sons'. My family educated me because I was their oldest son, while only one of my five sisters was sent to school – the only sister younger than me. All of my older sisters had to go to work from a young age to help support the family. A high school girlfriend of mine was offered a full college scholarship after graduation, but her parents didn't allow her to accept it because they wanted her to stay home and help them farm to raise money for her younger brother's junior high school fees. My own mom was never sent to school as a child, and she was married to my dad by the time she turned fifteen. Today, more than fifty per cent of my kitchen brigade is female, and I mentor any of my cooks who want to advance their skill. It is important, I feel, to uphold the inherited cultural norms that feel right and balanced for these modern times, while also letting go of some outdated norms that no longer serve us.

Finally, my hope is that this book offers a solid foundation for sustainable practices for our natural edible resources, as well as to retain our cherished Balinese food culture. As Bali continues to transform from an agrarian island to an island with expanding tourism, it's as important as ever to preserve our tegals (food forests) and fish and marine diversity. We need to keep our waterways clean, practice zero waste as much as possible and cook only what we will consume with renewable resources, such as bamboo, coconut husks and clay. Our culinary heritage holds a lot of the answers to the question: 'How could we be eating for a healthy, sustainable future?' May this book inspire us to try. I hope that readers enjoy diving into this book as much as we enjoyed making it.

GLOSSARY

There are some ingredients that are essential for Balinese cooking. Most can be found at good Asian grocers and supermarkets, but others might be difficult to track down overseas and may have to be substituted. For a guide to rare edible plants, see page 127.

AMARANTH LEAVES (BAYAM)

Fresh green bayam or amaranth leaves are similar to spinach in texture, with a sweeter, more distinct flavour. We use them in Ledok-ledok (page 203). Find them at select greengrocers or online.

BANANA LEAVES (DON BIU)

Banana leaves are the plates, cling-wrap, baking paper and doilies of Balinese kitchens. We use them to cook food, serve food, cover food and decorate the dining space. While some cooks swap them out for aluminium foil, we don't recommend doing this unless you're making Bebek betutu (page 238). The leaves can tear when you fold them against the grain, so remember to use the veins of the leaf as a guide, going with them, not against them (see guide page 27). Asian supermarkets and Thai grocers will often have fresh and frozen banana leaves. If you use frozen leaves, simply defrost them at room temperature when you start cooking. They take around 15 minutes to defrost and can be used in the same way as fresh leaves once they're ready.

BANANA TREE BLOSSOM (PUSUH)

In Bali, we consume many parts of the banana plant – the trunk (see page 127), fruit (see on right) and flowers. The blossoms, known locally as pusuh, are smooth, waxy and bouncy. When they're finely sliced, they make for a lovely urab ingredient (see page 132). Just remember to toss them with a good pinch of salt before cooking to extract the bitter sap. Most good Asian supermarkets or grocers stock banana blossoms and you can also order them online.

BANANAS (BIU)

All bananas are not made equal when it comes to Balinese cooking. Many varieties of the fruit are incorporated into different sweets and offerings. Generally speaking, the hardier the banana, the more suitable it is for cooking. There is the gedang saba (saba banana) variety that is short, plump and boiled as a snack with the skins on, battered and boiled into Pisang rai (page 168), or fried into Godoh (page 227). The longer biu raja banana receives a similar treatment and is also commonly used in traditional sweets. Some bananas, such as the super-sweet and soft biu susu, are reserved for eating fresh; others, such as biu sabit and biu ketip, need to be boiled before they're eaten. One particularly interesting variety, biu batu, is temptingly sweet but peppered with hard stones and is sometimes sliced into rujak. If you're overseas, you can use ladyfinger bananas or saba bananas. Shop for them at Asian supermarkets or grocers.

CANDLENUTS (TINGKIH/KEMIRI)

Candlenuts are waxy and have subtle, smoky undertones. They're used to thicken and bind spice pastes and not so much for their flavour. Most Asian supermarkets, organic grocers and good spice shops stock them, and you can also buy them online. You could also substitute them with their relative, the macadamia nut. Please note that candlenuts are mildly toxic when they're raw and should be cooked before consumption (see page 26).

CARUM (KEMANGI)
Carum leaves, also called kemangi and lemon basil, are used to perfume seafood dishes. If required, substitute with Thai basil.

CASSAVA (SELA KUTUH)
These calcium-rich roots with their firm white insides are steamed or roasted and served as a snack. In the drier parts of Bali they are used to replace rice as a starch. You can find cassava roots at most good supermarkets and greengrocers. If you don't have any luck there, try an Asian or African grocer. The leaves are used in many vegetable dishes and have a fresh, vibrant, chlorophyll-rich flavour. The leaves might be harder to come by, but some specialist suppliers can order them in. In recipes such as Bebek betutu (page 238) you can replace them with kale.

CASSUMUNAR GINGER (BANGLE)
A bright-yellow member of the ginger family that is used to bring depth, warmth and spice to some spice formulas, such as Base wangen (page 54). It's related to galangal and is deeply medicinal, with anti-parasitic, anti-inflammatory and antibacterial properties.

CHAYOTE (LABU SIAM)
Chayote, or choko, is a sweet green gourd that grows quickly and abundantly in the tropical heat. In Bali, it's mainly used in soups and broths for texture and sweetness. You'll find it at Asian grocers and good supermarkets, and it can be replaced with green papaya (see page 276), which has a similar gentle sweetness and gelatinous consistency.

CHILLIES (TABIA)
We use fresh green and red cabai rawit (or tabasco chillies) for heat, and larger Lombok chillies for flavour. If you can't find tabasco chillies, substitute them with Thai or bird's eye chillies, keeping in mind that bird's eye chillies are more compact and therefore a little more powerful than tabasco chillies, so you may want to reduce the number of chillies by one for every five if you choose to cook with this variety. Lombok chillies are larger and longer with a milder, sweeter flavour and a gentler heat that takes a while to kick in. They can be replaced with Fresno peppers, long Thai chillies or Anaheim peppers. Jarred or dried chillies and chilli flakes are not suitable for Balinese cooking. In Bali, we normally incorporate the whole chilli into a dish, so there's no need to remove the seeds.

COCONUT MILK (SANTEN)
Santen (page 94) is grated coconut that is squeezed together with water to create coconut milk. We strongly recommend you make your own santen for the recipes in this book. If you don't have time or can't find fresh coconuts, you can

use a tinned variety, but remember it won't match the fresh stuff in flavour, consistency or subtlety. The beauty of homemade santen is that it doesn't contain any preservatives or thickeners. If you are going for tinned coconut milk, be sure to test out a few varieties and select the brand with the highest fat and coconut content and the least amount of water, thickeners, additives and preservatives. Always go for full fat, avoid the watered-down light (or lite) varieties, and try to find a brand that does not contain added sugar. We like the brands Ayam and Chaokoh.

COCONUT OIL (LENGIS NYUH)
The best Balinese food is always cooked in homemade coconut oil (see page 97). If you're using store-bought coconut oil, shop around for virgin coconut oil and find a brand that is made from Indonesian coconuts, which are sweeter and earthier than, say, Thai coconuts. Vegetable oil, such as grapeseed, rice bran or sunflower oil, can be used as a very last resort substitute.

COCONUT WATER (AIR KELAPA)
The clear liquid inside young and old coconuts is known as coconut water (not to be confused with coconut milk). In Bali, we use the flesh and water from young coconuts in drinks and some desserts. Their juice and flesh is sweet and full of electrolytes, which also makes them a wonderful natural remedy for upset stomachs and dehydration. It is always best to use fresh young coconuts. We don't recommend using store-bought or packaged varieties. For instructions on how to open coconuts, see page 91.

COCONUTS (NYUH)
The coconut, as we have written about on pages 91–2, sits alongside roots and spices as one of the key players of the Balinese kitchen. Many Balinese recipes require coconut sugar, coconut milk and fresh mature coconut, which is often roasted and almost always grated (see pages 91–2 for a guide on how to open, prepare and roast coconuts) then used to uplift meat or vegetables. For cooked dishes, always use the older coconuts with the brown, hard shells – sometimes husks – on the outside. Avoid the shelled, bleached white variety sold in most supermarkets. Dried or desiccated coconut is not a suitable substitute in any of the recipes in this book. Young coconuts are only used for beverages and some iced desserts.

DALUMAN LEAVES
These cool, earthy, arrowhead-shaped leaves are hand-squeezed and left to set into a soft jelly that's often served in coconut milk as a dessert called Daluman (page 266). There's really no substitute for them, and they can be difficult to find outside Indonesia, but if you can't find them you can leave them out. Even within Bali itself, they are normally foraged from wild areas or tegals (food forests, see page 125).

FIDDLEHEAD FERN TIPS (PAKU)

Wild-grown and foraged fiddlehead ferns are a staple vegetable in the paon. We only use fresh, bouncy young tips, not the stalks, which are quite hard and stringy. The young tips of this mineral-rich vegetable are sweet and delicate with an interesting squeakiness to them. They are an extremely popular vegetable, often sautéed, chopped and tossed with grated coconut and spices in dishes such as urab (see page 132) and sometimes even battered and fried. Some greengrocers supply them and you can order them online. Try and get the freshest fern tips you can find, as they get quite sticky and gluey when they're old.

GALANGAL (ISEN)

A beautiful relative of ginger with a distinctly ringed, pink-tinged exterior and bright-white insides, galangal is used extensively in Balinese cooking for its earthiness and ability to refine other flavours. It pairs particularly well with pale meats like seafood, pork and poultry. Galangal is quite easy to find outside Indonesia at good supermarkets and Asian grocers. You can use frozen galangal, just make sure it's well thawed overnight (whole) before it's cooked.

JACKFRUIT (NANGKA)

Both ripe and unripe jackfruit are widely consumed in Bali. Young, or unripe jackfruit makes its way into stews such as Jukut nangka (page 151) and some lawars (see page 240). The ripe fruit is eaten on its own or diced and tossed into desserts. Young jackfruit is becoming an increasingly popular meat substitute across the globe and is therefore becoming easier to find in Asian grocers and some good supermarkets and greengrocers. It's mildly flavoured, so it is perfect for soaking up spices, and it has the meaty, almost stringy texture of pork when it's slow-cooked. When shopping for young jackfruit, look for fruits that are smaller with green–pale yellow skins and no aroma. Some cooks recommend replacing fresh unripe jackfruit with the tinned variety, but we feel it lacks in texture.

JAVANESE LONG PEPPERS (TABIA BUN)

These fragrant peppers (*Piper retrofractum*) are used for spice and heat, and the leaves are used as a vegetable. Medicinally, tabia bun is classed as an energy stimulant that warms the body, aids circulation and helps relieve stress. Fresh tabia bun leaves might be hard to find outside Indonesia, but you can buy the dried peppers from spice specialists. If you're in Australia, try Herbies (www.herbies.com.au).

JICAMA (BENGKUANG)

Jicama is a root vegetable with a thick brown skin and a sweet, white inside that makes for a refreshing addition to rujak (see page 165). Texturally, it's like a cross between a raw potato and a watermelon – crunchy, bouncy and packed with moisture. You can find it at Mexican specialty stores, Asian supermarkets and some conventional supermarkets.

LEMONGRASS (SERE)

Zesty, zingy lemongrass makes its way into many spice pastes, such as Base genep (page 50), and sambals, such as Sambal matah (page 76). Sometimes it's thrown into the likes of Nasi kuning (page 112) for aroma, or infused into medicinal tonics, such as Loloh kunyit (page 265), for its myriad medicinal properties – anxiety, infection and high-blood-pressure prevention among them. Most of the time, the hard, woody parts of the stem and leaves are chopped off, leaving the pale, fleshy sections for consumption. These will either be very finely chopped, or bruised and knotted (see page 28) and added to dishes as they cook for perfume. Lemongrass is widely available at conventional supermarkets and Asian grocers. If you're buying lemongrass in bulk, you can keep it in the freezer for 3–6 months.

LESSER GALANGAL (CEKUH)

Sometimes called aromatic ginger, or kencur in Indonesian, this is one of the most important spices of the Balinese kitchen, favoured for its sweetness, gentle heat and distinct perfume. It's in almost every savoury dish and cannot be omitted or replaced. It's also great for curing coughs. It can be difficult to find outside Indonesia, but some Asian supermarkets might sell it frozen or as a powder. You could also try looking on Amazon. If you are using a powder, substitute the amount of fresh lesser galangal with a third of its weight in powder (3:1 ratio), but remember: no more than one fresh ingredient should be substituted with a powder.

LIMES AND LIME LEAVES (JERUK LIMO, DON LIMO)

Lime is often the crowning element of a Balinese dish. A slice of the fruit is frequently used to finish a dish, and the juices are squeezed over the top just before serving. Lime leaves, too, are often very finely sliced and used as a powerful, zingy garnish. A few different kinds of lime work for Balinese cooking. Many cooks use the fruits and leaves of small jeruk limo limes (*Citrus amblycarpa*), others use makrut limes (limau in Indonesian). Jeruk limo are considerably smaller than regular limes, so cooks will often just cut them in half before garnishing a dish, but if you're using regular limes, quarter them. Makrut lime is sweeter with a more distinct perfume, so use it sparingly. If you're in Australia or the US, you can find makrut limes at select greengrocers. If limo or makrut limes are not available, regular limes and lime leaves are a fine substitute.

LIMESTONE PASTE (KAPUR SIRIH)

Kapur sirih is a white, chalk-like paste derived from limestone that is often used as a binder. In fried foods it helps crisp the batter and in boiled or poached foods, such as Pisang rai (page 168), it helps the batter thicken and congeal. You'll find it at Asian grocers and online.

MANGO (POH)

Many varieties of heirloom mangoes spring up in different parts of Bali. Some are used for medicinal purposes, such as reducing heat in the body, and others are purely grown to eat raw or ripe. Unripe green fruits are served in rujak (see page 165) and sambals. Some types of mango leaves can also be used as vegetables. They're grassy, slightly bitter and work well in salads with spices and coconut. Green mangoes can be found at most Asian supermarkets and grocers. They should be solid, aroma-free and light green in colour. For the recipes in this book, it doesn't really matter what kind of variety you buy as long as it's sour. Speak to your grocer for guidance.

PALM SUGAR (GULA BALI)

In Bali, cooks from different parts of the island use different kinds of palm sugar, depending on the kind of trees they are surrounded by. They could be using the sweeter, darker sugar of the coconut palm, the more savoury lontar (palmyra palm sugar) or gula aren (jaka palm sugar), the lightest in both colour and flavour. For the recipes in the From the Land chapter, we recommend using coconut palm sugar, and in the recipes in the From the Sea chapter, play around with lontar sugar if you can find it. Palm sugar is sold in blocks and is almost always grated or finely chopped, so avoid granulated palm sugar unless the recipe lists it specifically. Most supermarkets and all Asian grocers stock palm sugar of some variety.

PANDAN LEAVES (DAUN PANDAN)

Pandan leaves are used to perfume and add colour to savoury and sweet dishes. The colour extracted from pandan leaves is a bright, almost electric green – although none of the recipes in this book call for this. Flavour-wise, pandan leaves add a unique breed of depth and sweetness – they can almost taste smoky. Most Asian grocers sell fresh and dried leaves, but we strongly recommend fresh. Frozen leaves can be used as a last resort, just make sure they're completely thawed before you use them.

PAPAYA (GEDANG)

Ripe papaya is consumed as a fruit, but in the Balinese kitchen, both the young green fruits and leaves of the papaya tree are treated as vegetables. When you're shopping for green papaya to go into Urab gedang (page 204), look for smaller fruits that are hard to the touch, with bright-green skins and no noticeable perfume. Most Asian grocers will stock green papaya.

PEPPER (MICA)

Before chillies were introduced by Portuguese traders in the 16th century, pepper was the heat-bringer of choice in Balinese cooking. We mostly use white pepper for its milder flavour and colour, as it's sweeter, aromatic and less overpowering. See also Javanese long pepper (page 275).

RAMBUTANS (BULUAN)

Used in dishes such as Nyoman's rujak (page 165), rambutans are small tropical fruits with bright-red furry skins (hence the name buluan, which is derived from the word 'bulu', meaning hair) and sweet, fleshy translucent insides, almost reminiscent of a lychee. Asian grocers may stock rambutans, but if you can't find them you could replace with fresh lychees or longans.

RED (ASIAN) SHALLOTS (BAWANG MERAH)

The tiny red shallots (officially known as *Allium ascalonicum*) that we cook with in Bali have red skins, purple-tinged insides and a warm, sweet flavour. Outside Indonesia they're known as red Asian shallots and are smaller and rounder than eschallots. Look for them at Asian supermarkets and greengrocers. If you can't find them, they can be replaced with eschallots.

RICE (BERAS)

Balinese rice is generally medium-grained with sweet, grassy notes and a light, fluffy texture – not as loose as basmati or as sticky as, say, Japanese rice. If you don't have access to Indonesian rice, jasmine rice is a good substitute. Red rice also works well with most dishes, apart from Nasi kuning (page 112). Javara (www.javara.co.id) is a great source for a variety of heritage Indonesian rice varieties. Contact them to find out if they distribute near you.

SALAM LEAVES (DAUN SALAM)

There's really no substitute for salam leaves, also known as Indonesian bay leaves (not to be mistaken with regular bay leaves). The leaves more closely resemble curry leaves and are used to add depth and spice to stews, meats and sometimes even steamed rice. Although regular bay leaves are sometimes recommended as a substitute, they don't taste the same at all. Some Asian grocers and online suppliers sell dried salam leaves – use 1 dry leaf for every 3 fresh leaves. If you can't find them, just leave them out.

SALT (UYAH)

Bali's north and east coastlines are famous for their sea salt, which is still being produced the old-school way, by scooping water from the ocean and pouring it into evaporating beds made from earth or sometimes coconut wood. This method makes for extremely natural salt that's coarse, chemical-free and powerfully flavoured. We recommend using a coarse, natural sea salt as much as possible. Avoid fine salts or pink salts if you can.

SHRIMP PASTE (TERASI)

Most supermarkets and Asian grocers stock terasi, a paste made from small shrimps combined with sea salt and fermented in blocks in the sun. It's pungent, fishy-tasting and makes for a powerful seasoning in many sambals and spice pastes, such as rujaks (see page 165) and Pindang sambal tomat (page 200). It's normally roasted before it's used, which reduces the intensity and smell of the fresh product. If you really can't find any, have a shellfish allergy or don't like the flavour, it's usually okay to leave it out – it's mainly there for umami and punch. Terasi is seriously pungent, so be mindful of this when you're storing it (in the fridge, of course); a sealed container is a must.

SOURSOP (SIRSAK)

Strikingly shaped and scented, sirsak is an Indonesian dessert staple. This large, spiked fruit is often peeled, seeded and then blended into juices, torn and tossed into iced delicacies or used as a rujak ingredient (see page 165). Soursop is available at Asian grocers and supermarkets. When you're choosing your fruit, make sure the skin is green but slightly soft to the touch. The pulp on the inside should be white, not brown, and the aroma should be fresh and bright, not fermented.

STAR FRUIT AND BILIMBI (BELIMBING)

Belimbing, or star fruit, are long, curiously angled fruits that become perfectly star-shaped when they're sliced. In this book we use them in Nyoman's rujak (page 165). They have bright-yellow insides and verge on the line between sweet and tart. There's no real substitute, but you can find them at many Asian grocers. Bilimbi, on the other hand, are the smaller, rounder, sourer cousins of star fruit. We use them to bring tartness to dishes like Pepes be pasih (page 187). They can be replaced with green tomatoes.

TAMARIND (ASAM)

Tamarind is used to bring sourness or tartness to some Balinese dishes, namely desserts or drinks such as Loloh kunyit (page 265). Most dishes that call for tamarind only require a very small amount. Blocks of tamarind pulp and jars of tamarind paste are sold at Asian grocers, good supermarkets and online. We recommend using pulp, especially for recipes such as rujak (see page 165).

TARO (KELADI)

These corms, which are often mistaken for roots, are steamed or roasted and served as a snack with Gula Bali palm syrup (page 98), a good pinch of sea salt and grated coconut. Taro corms come from the striking *Colocasia esculenta* plant, known for its large elephant ear–shaped leaves. The corms have an interesting texture, starchier than sweet potato, with a much subtler flavour and bright-white centres. If you can't find fresh taro, use white yams or cassava instead. If you're in Australia, many good produce markets and Asian grocers sell taro.

TEMPE

Only use soybean tempe for the recipes in this book, and make sure it's plain soybean tempe – without any flavours or extra ingredients, such as wheat or other grains. Tempe is very easy to find overseas – look for it in the refrigerated section of your Asian grocer or supermarket.

TORCH GINGER FLOWERS (KECICANG OR KECOMBRANG)

These vibrantly pink blooms are sometimes referred to as bongkot, but this is actually the correct term for the stem of the plant, which is also used in Balinese cooking. Torch ginger springs abundantly from the island's verdant central regions. It has long, bright-green leaves and bright-magenta flowers, which are highly aromatic and are used to bring punch and vibrancy to sambals. They have an extremely unique flavour – almost pungent and a little bit peppery – and are deeply perfumed. There's no real substitute for them, but you can find them fresh at very good Asian grocers and online. Frozen can be used as a very last resort, but make sure you allow the flowers to thaw for at least 6 hours if they are whole.

TURMERIC (KUNYIT)

Turmeric is a highly prized anti-inflammatory plant in Balinese cooking and medicine. Turmeric roots are quite easy to find outside Indonesia these days, and Asian grocers and good supermarkets sell the fresh stuff. If you can't find fresh roots, you can use powder. Substitute the amount of fresh turmeric with a third of its weight in powder (3:1 ratio), but remember: no more than one fresh ingredient should be substituted with a powder. In some parts of Bali, turmeric leaves are also used as a wrapping or to add aroma to a dish (see page 129). If you can't access fresh leaves, omit them.

INDEX

ACKNOWLEDGEMENTS

Maya

Thank you Anak Agung Rai, my niang, for being the main source of inspiration behind these pages. And to my late grandfather, Tjokorda Ngurah, for bestowing your knowledge from above.

To my mother and father, Tjokorda Raka and Asri Kerthyasa, thank you for raising me so gracefully between two worlds. And to my wonderful brothers, Tjok Gde and Tjok Bagus, for supporting me endlessly throughout the process of making this book.

To Jero Mangku Gede Yudiawan, Kentri Norberg, Nyoman Darti and Keplus, thank you for sharing your kitchens and your cooking with us.

This book wouldn't exist without the encouragement, mentorship and support of my former editors Pat Nourse and Anthea Loucas. Pat and Ant, you are like family to me. I am extremely grateful for everything.

Jane Adams, Mila Shwaiko, Pete Keen, Will Goldfarb and Kim Herben – your friendship and guidance has been invaluable. Thank you. I would also like to salute I Made Pung, Ida Bagus Gangga and I Komang Latra for the knowledge you shared that made its way into the pages of this book.

Patricia Gillespie, thank you for sending me kisses and hugs from afar when I needed them.

Ronald Akili and the Potato Head family, your support has meant the world to us – which leads me to my collaborator, Wayan Kresna Yasa. Thank you for joining forces with me and imparting your stories, recipes and experiences into the pages of this book. Mary Kresna Yasa, thanks for being an integral part of our journey.

Thank you Martin Westlake for your beautiful images and for joining us on our adventures. Jane Willson and Anna Collett, I express my deepest gratitude for believing in Paon and giving us a platform to share our love of Balinese cooking with the world. Helena Holmgren and George Saad, thank you for all the work you've done to bring this book to life.

My dear Lucas, you inspire me to record everything I have learnt for the generations to come. May you grow to become a true custodian of this planet through your culture.

And to the invisible powers that drove the creation of Paon – the elements, the spirit guardians, the whispers from the Universe – I humbly give thanks for being granted your permission to communicate this information, which at its essence is divine wisdom bestowed upon us by you.

Wayan

Paon would not be possible without the endless support and encouragement from my family. Thank you to my wife, Mary Kresna Yasa, who always has my back and loves me in that steadfast, soulmate kind of way. It is you who taught me that life can be limitless and dreams are only dreams until we wake up. To my father and mother, thank you for bringing me into this world and letting me do what I love to do. My work ethic and camaraderie with the land and sea are from you. Janet Whittington, the best mother-in-law, the one whose confidence in me does not waver, I am honoured to be your 'new strong son'.

To Maya Kerthyasa, thank you for your true passion to champion Balinese cuisine on the global stage, and for being the first to propose we write a dedicated book on it. We did it!

Thanks to Hardie Grant for the opportunity to bring Paon to life. To the entire team that helped make it happen: Jane Willson, Anna Collett, Helena Holmgren, George Saad and Martin Westlake, thank you for believing in us and making it beautiful.

My heartfelt gratitude goes out to all of the chefs who have, in one way or another, helped to make Paon possible: Dan Barber, for teaching me that flavour begins before any seed is planted; Will Goldfarb, for believing in me and bringing me back to Bali; Daryl Wonoraharjo, the loyal wingman who promises, 'gue amanin (I'm on top of it)'; Oka Widiasa, who guides me and teaches me about real Balinese cuisine; and Antoine Audran, the first chef to truly inspire me to explore Indonesian flavours, despite the fact that he himself was born in France!

To Ronald Akili and the Potato Head team – my dream when I became a chef was to bring Balinese and Indonesian cuisine to the far reaches of the world. You all, more than anybody or anything else, are the reasons this dream has been realised, beginning the moment you invited me to join the Kaum opening team. Let's keep shining that Indonesian light.

Big thanks to Jed Doble, one of the first in the local F&B scene to publicly recognise my work. Move over, Michelin and James Beard, nothing means more to me than being named 2018 Foodies Magazine Chef of the Year Bali! To my dear friend Billie Mintz, seeing myself through your eyes is a salve to my soul. Thank you for your vision, brother.

To Chef Yudhi at Dapur Bali Mula, and to all of the Balinese chefs, home cooks and priests keeping Balinese food heritage and culture alive for future generations: Matur suksma. It is because of you all that we still have stories to tell.

ABOUT THE AUTHORS

Tjok Maya Kerthyasa is an Indonesian-Australian writer living in Ubud, Bali. She spent just under a decade in Sydney writing for *Australian Gourmet Traveller* magazine before moving home to Bali to reconnect with her family and her motherland. Since returning home, Maya has hosted culinary-based events, starred in an Indonesian food-based web series called *Masakan Rumah* and spoken about Balinese cooking for various media platforms. Maya is documenting her grandmother's recipes to share with the next generation of Balinese cooks and food lovers from other parts of the world. Her mission is to see the cuisine better understood and celebrated on a global level.

I Wayan Kresna Yasa is a Balinese chef born on the island of Nusa Penida, off Bali's east coast. He trained and worked in the US for six years, cooking at the likes of Acadia in Chicago and New York's Blue Hill Stone Barns. In Bali, he is known for the deftness of his cooking, his deep respect for the environment and his drive to put the flavours of his home on the global culinary map. He helped launch Room4Dessert with chef-owner Will Goldfarb, before transitioning to the Indonesian lifestyle and hospitality group Potato Head. Wayan is now global executive chef and culinary director for the Potato Head family. He opened Ijen – the group's first zero-waste sustainable seafood restaurant – and Kaum, which is known for its revival of rare tribal recipes from across the archipelago. His most recent venture is plant-based restaurant Tanaman, which was listed as one of the best new restaurants in the world in *Condé Nast Traveller*'s June 2020 issue.

Published in 2022 by Hardie Grant Books,
an imprint of Hardie Grant Publishing

Hardie Grant Books (Melbourne)
Wurundjeri Country
Building 1, 658 Church Street
Richmond, Victoria 3121

Hardie Grant Books (London)
5th & 6th Floors
52–54 Southwark Street
London SE1 1UN

hardiegrantbooks.com

Hardie Grant acknowledges the Traditional Owners of the country
on which we work, the Wurundjeri people of the Kulin nation and the
Gadigal people of the Eora nation, and recognises their continuing
connection to the land, waters and culture. We pay our respects to their
Elders past and present.

All rights reserved. No part of this publication may be reproduced,
stored in a retrieval system or transmitted in any form by any means,
electronic, mechanical, photocopying, recording or otherwise, without
the prior written permission of the publishers and copyright holders.

The moral rights of the authors have been asserted.

Copyright text © Tjok Maya Kerthyasa and I Wayan Kresna Yasa 2022
Copyright photography © Martin Westlake 2022, except page 271
(on right) © Billie Mintz 2022
Copyright illustrations © Tjok Maya Kerthyasa 2022
Copyright design © Hardie Grant Publishing 2022

 A catalogue record for this
book is available from the
National Library of Australia

Paon

ISBN 9781 74379 753 2

10 9 8 7 6 5 4 3 2 1

Publishing Director: Jane Willson
Project Editor: Anna Collett
Editor: Helena Holmgren
Design Manager: Kristin Thomas
Designer: George Saad
Photographer: Martin Westlake
Production Manager: Todd Rechner

Colour reproduction by Splitting Image Colour Studio
Printed in China by Leo Paper Products LTD.

The paper this book is printed on is from FSC®-certified forests and
other sources. FSC® promotes environmentally responsible, socially
beneficial and economically viable management of the world's forests.